Praise for Michael E. Gerber, Norbert C. Lemermeyer, and *The E-Myth Architect*

Lemermeyer's legacy of the strong and classic architectural practice transcends to meet millennium culture in this open, honest and brave treatise exposing the not-so-glamorous operations of running an architectural practice.

Norbert shares the insights of 30 years' experience and the common denominators that affect all business owners on the journey to establish a successful, profitable architectural business.

This book is both inspirational and healing as it triggers the kindred spirit of change within deeply rooted architectural ritual and practice.

Sherri Shorten, Architect AAA, M.Arch, Edmonton, Canada

I have completed photographic assignments for many architects throughout Western Canada and seen the inner workings and struggles of my clients' business operations. I say to them:

Evolve or struggle endlessly. *The E-Myth Architect* is an essential book for all architects in business today. It will make you laugh, cry and ultimately cheer. Embrace the wisdom in this book and you and your practice will be transformed.

Robert Lemermeyer, Photographer, Calgary, Canada

Norbert Lemermeyer in *The E-Myth Architect* picks up on what architecture schools neglect to teach. He demonstrates a hands-on approach to making it in the business world of architecture!

Mindy Gudzinski, M.Arch, BEDS, BA, MRAIC, Edmonton, Canada

An architect's formal education glosses over the need to treat our fledgling professional practice as a real business. We are taught in true Howard Roark fashion (of *The Fountainhead* fame) to simply concentrate on our design abilities and all the other pieces of the practice puzzle will fall neatly into place. Today, hard work, luck and even design talent are no longer enough to make an architectural practice work, let alone succeed and prosper over time.

In the *The E-Myth Architect*, Norbert Lemermeyer writes from hard-learned experience. He offers us insights into what it takes to plan, launch and refine an architectural practice that can work effectively in today's competitive reality.

When I started my own practice over thirty years ago, I naively thought good, competent design and "people skills" would be enough to succeed. In reality, a successful firm requires much, much more. If we are to grow, prosper and thrive in our business of architecture, we have to envision the kind of practice that will work best for us. If we don't spend the time asking ourselves the tough questions, we are doomed to letting our practices run us. As Norbert says: we end up "doing it, doing it" rather than "planning it." So true.

The E-Myth Architect leads us step by step through the process of planning and creating our own business/practice plan. Norbert shows us how to really engage and work with a client to create a strong, long-lasting relationship, rather than falling into the trap of just designing another building. He offers real world advice on staffing, marketing, finances, time management and most importantly, our own personal growth.

The business of architecture requires you to formulate and follow your own unique vision. *The E-Myth Architect* will help you find your way to a more rewarding and fulfilling practice

Richard Vanderwell, M.Arch, Architect, Edmonton, Canada

Like my friend and colleague Norbert Lemermeyer, I too was profoundly changed when I read Michael E. Gerber's book, *The E-Myth*. However, unlike Norbert, who actually did something about it and radically changed the way he practiced architecture, I changed some little things but never truly embraced what Gerber was saying. But now, having read *The E-Myth Architect*, I am excited by what I can do and when I do it, I too, will give this book to another architect and say, "Read, re-read it; it changed my life forever … enjoy."

Terry Hartwig, MAAA, MRAIC, Edmonton, Canada

Having practiced Architecture for the same period as Norbert, I was amazed at how many parallels I have experienced that were described in these chapters. The most important principle that I got from reading the chapters by Norbert is that it has to be a business first, and that means keeping most of your feelings out of it.

If the proper systems are in place, so that the roles, duties, and standards are all defined, it then allows the procedure or process to maintain its pace to an effective, efficient and profitable result. I strongly encourage all to read this book before establishing their own practice or becoming a part of an organization. You will begin to understand the business of the business. This book offers and provides a practical and professional approach to making your pursuit successful.

Derek Haight, B.Arch, MAAA, MRAIC, Calgary, Canada

Michael Gerber's *E-Myth* is one of only four books I recommend as required reading. **For those looking to start and build a business of their own, this is the man who has coached more successful entrepreneurs than the next ten gurus combined.**

Timothy Ferris, #1 *New York Times* best-selling author, *The 4-Hour Workweek*

Everyone needs a mentor, someone who tells it like it is, holds you accountable, and shows you your good, bad, and ugly. For millions of small-business owners, Michael Gerber is that person. Let Michael be your mentor and you are in for a kick in the pants, the ride of a lifetime.

John Jantsch, author, *Duct Tape Marketing*

Michael Gerber is a master instructor and a leader's leader. As a combat F15 fighter pilot, I had to navigate complex missions with life-and-death consequences, but until I read *The E-Myth* and met Michael Gerber, my transition to the world of small business was a nightmare with no real flight plan. **The hands-on, practical magic of Michael's turnkey systems magnified by the raw power of his keen insight and wisdom have changed my life forever.**

Steve Olds, CEO, Stratworx.com

Michael Gerber's strategies in *The E-Myth* were instrumental in building my company from two employees to a global organization; I can't wait to see how applying the strategies from *Awakening the Entrepreneur Within* will affect its growth!

Dr. Ivan Misner, founder and chairman, BNI; author, *Masters of Sales*

Michael Gerber's gift to isolate the issues and present simple, direct, business-changing solutions shines bright with *Awakening the Entrepreneur Within*. **If you're interested in developing an entrepreneurial vision and plan that inspires others to action, buy this book, read it, and apply the processes Gerber brilliantly defines.**

Tim Templeton, author, *The Referral of a Lifetime*

Michael Gerber truly, truly understands what it takes to be a successful practicing entrepreneur and business owner. He has demonstrated to me over six years of working with him that for those who stay the course and learn much more than just "how to work on their business and not in it" then they will reap rich rewards. **I finally franchised my business, and the key to unlocking this kind of potential in any business is the teachings of Michael's work.**

Chris Owen, marketing director, Royal Armouries (International) PLC

Michael's work has been an inspiration to us. **His books have helped us get free from the out-of-control life that we once had. His no-nonsense approach kept us focused on our ultimate aim rather than day-to-day stresses. He has helped take our business to levels we couldn't have imagined possible. In the Dreaming Room made us totally reevaluate** how we thought about our business and our life. We have now redesigned our life so we can manifest the dreams we unearthed in Michael's Dreaming Room.

Jo and Steve Davison, founders, The Spinal Health Clinic
Chiropractic Group and www.your-dream-life.com

Because of Michael Gerber, I transformed my twenty-four-hour-a-day, seven-day-a-week job (also called a small business) into a multi-million dollar turnkey business. This in turn set the foundation for my worldwide training firm. **I am living my dream because of Michael Gerber.**

Howard Partridge, Phenomenal Products Inc.

Michael Gerber is an outrageous revolutionary who is changing the way the world does business. **He dares you to commit to your grandest dreams and then shows you how to make the impossible a reality. If you let him, this man will change your life.**

Fiona Fallon, founder, Divine and The Bottom Line

Michael Gerber is a genius. Every successful business person I meet has read Michael Gerber, refers to Michael Gerber, and lives by his words. You just can't get enough of Michael Gerber. **He has the innate (and rare) ability to tap into one's soul, look deeply, and tell you what you need to hear. And then, he inspires you, equips you with the tools to get it done.**

Pauline O'Malley, CEO, TheRevenueBuilder

When asked, "Who was the most influential person in your life?" I am one of the thousands who don't hesitate to say "Michael E. Gerber." **Michael helped transform me from someone dreaming of retirement to someone dreaming of working until age one hundred.** This awakening is the predictable outcome of anyone reading Michael's new book.

Thomas O. Bardeen

Michael Gerber is an incredible business philosopher, guru, perhaps even a seer. He has an amazing intuition, which allows him to see in an instant what everybody else is missing; he sees opportunity everywhere. **While in the Dreaming Room, Michael gave me the gift of seeing through the eyes of an awakened entrepreneur, and instantly my business changed from a regional success to serving clients on four continents.**

Keith G. Schiehl, president, Rent-a-Geek Computer Services

Michael Gerber is among the very few who truly understand entrepreneurship and small business. While others talk about these topics in the form of theories, methodologies, processes, and so on, Michael goes to the heart of the issues. **Whenever Michael writes about entrepreneurship, soak it in as it is not only good for your business, but great for your soul.** His words will help you to keep your passion and balance while sailing through the uncertain sea of entrepreneurship.

Raymond Yeh, co-author, *The Art of Business*

Michael Gerber forced me to think big, think real, and gave me the support network to make it happen. A new wave of entrepreneurs is rising, much in thanks to his amazing efforts and very practical approach to doing business.

Christian Kessner, founder, Higher Ground Retreats and Events

Michael's understanding of entrepreneurship and small business management has been a difference maker for countless businesses, including Infusion Software. **His insights into the entrepreneurial process of building a business are a must-read for every small business owner.** The vision, clarity, and leadership that came out of our Dreaming Room experience were just what our company needed to recognize our potential and motivate the whole company to achieve it.

Clate Mask, president and CEO, Infusion Software

Michael Gerber is a truly remarkable man. His steady openness of mind and ability to get to the deeper level continues to be an inspiration and encouragement to me. **He seems to always ask that one question that forces the new perspective to break open and he approaches the new coming method in a fearless way.**

Rabbi Levi Cunin, Chabad of Malibu

The Dreaming Room experience was literally life changing for us. **Within months, we were able to start our foundation and make several television appearances owing to his teachings.** He has an incredible charisma, which is priceless, but above all Michael Gerber *awakens* passion from within, enabling you to take action with dramatic results . . . starting today!

Shona and Shaun Carcary, Trinity Property Investments Inc. — Home Vestors franchises

I thought *E-Myth* was an awkward name! What could this book do for me? **But when I finally got to reading it . . . it was what I was looking for all along.** Then, to top it off, I took a twenty-seven-hour trip to San Diego just to attend the Dreaming Room, where Michael touched my heart, my mind, and my soul.

Helmi Natto, president, Eye 2 Eye Optics, Saudi Arabia

I attended In the Dreaming Room and was challenged by Michael Gerber to "Go out and do what's impossible." So I did. **I became an author and international speaker and used Michael's principles to create a world-class company that will change and save lives all over the world.**

Dr. Don Kennedy, MBA; author, *5 AM & Already Behind*, www.bahbits.com

I went to the Dreaming Room to have Michael Gerber fix my business. He talked about Dreaming. What was this Dreaming? I was too busy working! Too busy being miserable, angry, frustrated, behind in what I was trying to accomplish. And losing everything I was working for. **Then Michael Gerber woke up the dreamer in me and remade my life and my business.**

Pat Doorn, president, Mountain View Electric Ltd.

Michael Gerber can captivate a room full of entrepreneurs and take them to a place where they can focus on the essentials that are the underpinning of every successful business. He gently leads them from where they are to where they need to be in order to change the world.

Francine Hardaway, CEO, Stealthmode Partners; founder,
the Arizona Entrepreneurship Conferences

The E Myth

Architect

*Why Most Architectural
Firms Don't Work
and What to Do About It*

MICHAEL E. GERBER

NORBERT C. LEMERMEYER

PRODIGY
BUSINESS BOOKS

Published by
Prodigy Business Books, Inc., Carlsbad, California.

Production Team
Patricia Beaulieu, COO, Prodigy Business Books, Inc.; Michael Levin, editor; Erich Broesel, cover designer, BroeselDesign, Inc.; Nancy Ratkiewich, book production, njr productions; Jeff Kassebaum, Michael E. Gerber author photographer, Jeff Kassebaum and Co.; Norbert Lemermeyer co-author photographer, Robert Lemermeyer.

For general information on other products and services, please visit the website: www.michaelegerber.com.

ISBN 978-0-9835001-9-3 (cloth)
ISBN 978-0-9835542-4-0 (ebk)

Printed in the United States of America

10 9 8 7 6 5 4 3 2 1

To Luz Delia, whose heart expands mine,
whose soul inspires mine,
whose boldness reaches for the stars, thank you,
forever, for being, truly mine...

—Michael E. Gerber

CONTENTS

A Word About This Book   *iii*

A Note from Norbert   *v*

Preface   *ix*

Acknowledgments   *xiii*

Introduction   *xvii*

Chapter 1: The Story of Steve and Peggy   1

Chapter 2: The Love of Architecture   9

Chapter 3: On the Subject of Money   15

Chapter 4: Money in Perspective   27

Chapter 5: On the Subject of Planning   33

Chapter 6: Not Without Planning   43

Chapter 7: On the Subject of Management   53

Chapter 8: Seemingly Unmanageable   59

Chapter 9: On the Subject of People   67

Chapter 10: People Make It Happen   73

Chapter 11: On the Subject of Associates   85

Chapter 12: An Architect's View   89

Chapter 13: On the Subject of Estimating   95

Chapter 14: Is Anything Certain?   99

Chapter 15: On the Subject of Clients   105

Chapter 16: How Does Your Client Love You?   111

Chapter 17: On the Subject of Growth   117

Chapter 18: Growth Beyond Architecture   121

Chapter 19: On the Subject of Change   129

Chapter 20: Changes   137

Chapter 21: On the Subject of Time   145

Chapter 22: How Will You Spend Your Time?   151

Chapter 23: On the Subject of Work   157

Chapter 24: The Other Work   161

Chapter 25: On the Subject of Taking Action   165

Chapter 26: Taking Action   171

Afterword   177
About the Authors   179
About the Series   182

A WORD ABOUT THIS BOOK

Michael E. Gerber

My first E-Myth book was published in 1986. It was called *The E-Myth: Why Most Small Businesses Don't Work and What To Do About It.* Since that book, and the company I created to provide business development services to its many readers, millions have read *The E-Myth*, and the book that followed it called *The E-Myth Revisited*, and tens of thousands have participated in our E-Myth Mastery programs.

The co-author of this book, Norbert Lemermeyer, Architect AAA, MEvDes, MRAIC, is one of my more enthusiastic readers, and as a direct result of his enthusiasm, his architectural firm became one of those clients. He became, over the years, one of my friends.

This book is two things: the product of my lifelong work conceiving, developing, and growing the E-Myth way into a business model that has been applied to every imaginable kind of company in the world, as well as a product of Norbert's extraordinary experience and success applying the E-Myth to the development of his equally extraordinary enterprise.

So it was that one day, while sitting with my muse, which I think of as my inner voice, and which many who know me think of as "Here he goes again!" I thought about the creation of an entire series of E-Myth Expert books. That series, including this book, would be co-authored by experts in every industry who had successfully applied my E-Myth principles to the extreme development of a practice—a very small company—with the intent of growing it nationwide, and even worldwide, which is what Norbert had in mind as he began to discover the almost infinite range of opportunities provided by thinking the E-Myth way.

Upon seeing the possibilities of this new idea, I immediately invited co-authors such as Norbert to join me. They said, "Let's do it!" and so we did.

Welcome to *The E-Myth Architect: Why Most Architectural Firms Don't Work and What to Do About It.*

Read it, enjoy it, and let us—Norbert and I—help you apply the E-Myth to the re-creation, development, and extreme growth of your architectural firm into an enterprise that you can be justifiably proud of.

To your life, your wisdom, and the life and success of your clients, I wish you good reading.

—Michael E. Gerber
Co-Founder/Chairman
Michael E. Gerber Companies, Inc.
Carlsbad, California
www.michaelegerber.com/co-author

A NOTE FROM NORBERT

Reading this book and implementing its messages will transform the way you practice architecture, and in the process, may change your life. I am a practicing architect. In 1994, a business coach recommended a book by Michael E. Gerber: *The E-Myth: Why Most Small Business Don't Work and What To Do About It*. No one, except Michael E. Gerber, could have imagined what happened.

Prior to 1994, I had been in business for fifteen years. I bought the book and read it cover to cover. Unlike most business books, it was understandable and described exactly what was wrong in my business. Since my business was struggling, I decided that I had nothing to lose, and to follow the recommendations in the book and change the way I conducted my business affairs.

With the book's guidance, I knew what to do to change, having faith that the outcomes of my business would be different. I was then working "on the business" rather than "in the business." At first, this principle seemed to be a play on words, but each day, as I followed the advice on how to intentionally design, create, and mold the business, I began to experience its impact. Originally my firm was set up following the model of the firm I had worked for before starting on my own practice—the classic, old school model of an architectural office setup.

It didn't take long before the impact of the E-Myth methods began to bring in new customers. This happened before we had fully established the E-Myth culture of the new way of doing things. Because of all the new work, before I knew it, I had reverted to the old way of "working in the business." The business was financially successful; however, I was working every waking minute and began to hate my life. I had forgotten what *The E-Myth* had taught me about setting up a successful business. I began to hate my employees, my clients, my work, and myself.

In 2002, the only way that I knew how to get rid of my problem was to sell the business. After the sale, everything was going along fine. I had some hobbies, I traveled and had some interests outside architecture. Before long, I picked up a few small building design projects just to stay involved. It didn't take long before I was facing the same problems as when I ran a larger business. Somewhere inside me I imagined that there must be a way to practice architecture successfully without the long hours and frustrations.

So I went back to *The E-Myth* and reread it. Also, I visited the E-Myth web site where I learned about the E-Myth Mastery Program. This program gave me the details in all aspects of how to set up and operate a successful business. This program had, along with weekly instruction lessons, a coaching program where each week you could discuss questions and business-related problems. As I went through the program, I set up all aspects of the new company in accordance with E-Myth Mastery as they were concurrently covered in the program.

When I was about halfway through the program, an associate of mine invited me to join him in a newly established firm. I agreed, on the condition that the new firm would have to be set up to precisely follow the E-Myth Mastery Program and the E-Myth method of business. In 2007, we began, and now we are in our fourth year. We have taken the time necessary to set up all systems and processes properly, in keeping with the E-Myth model. Already the successful impact of an E-Myth architectural practice can be felt. We can see that down the road, the foundations have been set that will serve us in the long run to establish a firm that is both profitable and impactful in the community.

Now I again love my chosen profession, enjoy my colleagues, have developed great working relationships with my clients, enjoy going to work each day, and, most importantly, have long holidays and don't work on weekends. Because of the way the office is organized with systems and processes, it runs without my daily input. When I'm away for extended periods of times, the clients get service of a high quality standard. I came to understand that the practice of architecture as a business was something bigger than and, most importantly, separate from myself—a living entity that could be intentionally designed, molded, and created.

Over the years since my first introduction to the E-Myth, I have moved beyond merely understanding the message to living it day to day. With the E-Myth approach, the firm has been completely retooled to where we see no limit to what we can do. We've had feedback from clients, consultants, and others interfacing with our firm. They remark on our ability to stay on top of things, to complete our work on time, to meet deadlines, and to more effectively complete our work. We accomplish this with young technologists with little former experience.

As experienced architects, familiar with how architects think, we know some of you are already muttering that it is different for you and your architectural practice because … you fill in the blank. Believe me, I've heard every reason why these principles don't work in Canada, California, Montana, Quebec, Florida, or Toronto! I've heard it can't apply to a small architectural practice, a large practice, or a design-oriented practice. In fact, these timeless principles of the E-Myth work wonders in any locale for any size or kind of practice.

To benefit from this book, you've got to clear away all those old ideas that your practice is somehow different, because this type of thinking keeps most architects stuck in the daily grind of, as Michael E. Gerber says, "Doing it, doing it, and doing it." The real key is to start thinking of your practice as a business that provides architectural services. If you don't want a "business," then give this book to someone else. Make no mistake about it, this book is about business and, more specifically, about how you can turn your architectural practice into a business that ultimately has a life apart from you.

As an architect, I understand the evolution of the dream from the first day in the school of architecture. I understand how the dream peaked as I passed the professional practice exams and became a registered architect. I remember the heady days of living the dream in my early days of practice. And I understand the moment when my dream came face-to-face with the harsh reality of long hours, tedious paperwork, and the nonstop conflicts of running a practice. Unfortunately, after many years grinding it out, I also understand the all-too-common cynicism that replaces that dream. In fact, my dream that once was a guiding star is now just a distant and foolish memory.

The unique characteristic of architecture is that it is an honorable, professional practice, the combination of knowledge and experience, and the visionary of the built environment. An architect is always gaining more experience/expertise and adding it to his or her knowledge. That alone is a full-time job. However, an architect also needs the skills required to run a profitable architectural firm as it morphs into something more complex and exponentially more time-consuming. That's something no one ever taught me in architectural school.

So here I am down the road as an architect. In my case, I've had thirty-three years as a practicing architect. I've seen it all and know exactly what's needed to get you out of the unfulfilled practice trap. The initial guiding light was the book I read years ago. Now I join with Michael, as an E-Myth architect, to help you see the practice of architecture in a whole new light, from a revolutionary point of view.

If you are ready to be a serious student and fully commit to changing how you think about your practice, turn the pages and get ready for the ride of your life. Granted, this is by no means the final word on each of these topics, but it is a grand introduction to a new way of thinking. For me, the reading of the original E-Myth book was the defining moment in my business. I hope that this book will be as significant to you. "Read, Re-read, Enjoy!"

—Norbert C. Lemermeyer
Member of the Royal Architectural Institute of Canada &
Alberta Association of Architects
Edmonton, Alberta, Canada
www.michaelegerber.com/co-author

PREFACE

Michael E. Gerber

I am not an architect, though I have helped dozens of architects reinvent their architectural firms over the past thirty-five years.

I like to think of myself as a thinker, maybe even a dreamer. Yes, I like to *do* things. But before I jump in and get my hands dirty, I prefer to think through what I'm going to do and figure out the best way to do it. I imagine the impossible, dream big, and then try to figure out how the impossible can become the possible. After that, it's about how to turn the possible into reality.

Over the years, I've made it my business to study how things work and how people work—specifically, how things and people work best together to produce optimum results. That means creating an organization that can do great things and achieve more than any other organization can.

This book is about how to produce the best results as a real-world architect in the development, expansion, and *liberation* of your firm. In the process, you will come to understand what the practice of architecture—as a *business*—is, and what it isn't. If you keep focusing on what it isn't, you're destined for failure. But if you turn your sights on what it is, the tide will turn.

This book, intentionally small, is about big ideas. The topics we'll be discussing in this book are the very issues that architects face daily in their practice. You know what they are: money, management, clients, and many more. My aim is to help you begin the exciting process of totally transforming the way you do business. As such, I'm confident that *The E-Myth Architect* could well be the most important book on the practice of architecture as a business that you'll ever read.

Unlike other books on the market, my goal is not to tell you how to do the work you do. Instead, I want to share with you the E-Myth philosophy as a way to revolutionize the way you think about the work you do. I'm convinced that this new way of thinking is something architects everywhere must adopt in order for their architectural firm to flourish during these trying times. I call it strategic thinking, as opposed to tactical thinking.

In strategic thinking, also called systems thinking, you, the architect, will begin to think about your entire practice—the broad scope of it—instead of focusing on its individual parts. You will begin to see the end game (perhaps for the first time) rather than just the day-to-day routine that's consuming you—the endless, draining work I call "doing it, doing it, doing it."

Understanding strategic thinking will enable you to create a practice that becomes a successful business, with the potential to flourish as an even more successful enterprise. But in order for you to accomplish this, your firm, your business, and certainly your enterprise must work *apart* from you instead of *because* of you.

The E-Myth philosophy says that a highly successful architectural firm can grow into a highly successful architecture business, which in turn can become the foundation for an inordinately successful architecture enterprise that runs smoothly and efficiently *without* the architect having to be in the office for ten hours a day, six days a week.

So what is "The E-Myth," exactly? The E-Myth is short for the Entrepreneurial Myth, which says that most businesses fail to fulfill their potential because most people starting their own business are not entrepreneurs at all. They're actually what I call *technicians suffering from an entrepreneurial seizure.* When technicians suffering from an entrepreneurial seizure start an architectural firm of their own, they almost always end up working themselves into a frenzy; their days are booked solid with appointments, one client after another. These architects are burning the candle at both ends, fueled by too much coffee and too little sleep, and most of the time, they can't even stop to think.

In short, the E-Myth says that most architects don't own a true business—most own a job. They're doing it, doing it, doing it, hoping like hell to get some time off, but never figuring out how to get their business to run without them. And if your business doesn't run well without you, what happens when you can't be in two places at once? Ultimately, your practice will fail.

There are a number of prestigious schools throughout the world dedicated to teaching the science of architecture. The problem is they fail to teach the *business* of it. And because no one is being taught how to run a practice as a business, some architects find themselves having to close their doors every year. You could be a world-class expert in model architecture building, historic preservation of lands, electrical engineering, or blueprint design, but when it comes to building a successful business, all that specified knowledge matters exactly zilch.

The good news is that you don't have to be among the statistics of failure in the architecture profession. The E-Myth philosophy I am about to share with you in this book has been successfully applied to thousands of architectural firms just like yours with extraordinary results.

The key to transforming your practice—and your life—is to grasp the profound difference between going to work *on* your practice (systems thinker) and going to work *in* your practice (tactical thinker). In other words, it's the difference between going to work on your practice as an entrepreneur and going to work in your practice as an architect.

The two are not mutually exclusive. In fact, they are essential to each other. The problem with most architectural firms is that the systems thinker—the entrepreneur—is completely absent. And so is the vision.

The E-Myth philosophy says that the key to transforming your firm into a successful enterprise is knowing how to transform yourself from successful architect technician into successful technician-manager-entrepreneur. In the process, everything you do in your architectural firm will be transformed. The door is then open to turning it into the kind of practice it should be—a practice, a business, an enterprise of pure joy.

The E-Myth not only can work for you, it will work for you. In the process, it will give you an entirely new experience of your business and beyond.

To your future and your life. Good reading.

—Michael E. Gerber
Co-Founder/Chairman
Michael E. Gerber Companies, Inc.
Carlsbad, California
www.michaelegerber.com/co-author

ACKNOWLEDGMENTS

Michael E. Gerber

As always, and never to be forgotten, there are those who give of themselves to make my work possible.

To my dearest and most forgiving partner, wife, friend, and co-founder, Luz Delia Gerber, whose love and commitment takes me to places I would often not go unaccompanied.

To Michael Levin, without your Pulitzer mentality, knowledge and expertise as an editor, we couldn't have done it without you.

To Erich Broesel, our stand-alone graphic designer and otherwise visual genius who supported the creation of all things visual that will forever be all things Gerber, we thank you, deeply, for your continuous contribution of things both temporal and eternal.

To Trish Beaulieu, wow, you are splendid.

And to Nancy Ratkiewich, whose work has been essential for you who are reading this.

To Johanna Nilsson and Katie Wagner, social media extraordinaires who have shown me you can teach an old dog new tricks.

To those many, many dreamers, thinkers, storytellers, and leaders, whose travels with me in The Dreaming Room have given me life, breath, and pleasure unanticipated before we met. To those many participants in my life (you know who you are), thank you for taking me seriously, and joining me in this exhilarating quest.

And, of course, to my co-authors, all of you, your genius, wisdom, intelligence, and wit have supplied me with a grand view of the world, which would never have been the same without you.

Love to all.

ACKNOWLEDGMENTS

Norbert C. Lemermeyer

My deep gratitude to the business coach, friend, visionary, and client Bill Bagshaw, Focus Customer Development Group, Edmonton, Canada. Thanks again for insisting that I read *The E-Myth* book. Also, thanks to all of my colleagues in Edmonton who shared with me accounts of their struggles to maintain an architectural practice. Bea Bohm Meyer, a personal success coach, helped me overcome my fear of my employees when I took the leap to trusting them and challenging them to work in a systems environment. Finally, to Wayne H. Heartwell, who, along with me, had the courage to change the way our services are delivered and bring the E-Myth vision to life.

INTRODUCTION

Michael E. Gerber

A s I write this book, the recession continues to take its toll on American businesses. Like any other industry, architecture is not immune. Architects all over the country are watching as homeowners are putting off remodeling, refurnishing, and home adjustments. At a time when per capita disposable income is at an all-time low, many home and business owners are choosing not to spend their hard-earned money on architectural and engineering services for themselves, their businesses, and their own families. As a result, architectural redesign, especially for deteriorating properties, moves from the realm of necessary for rebuilding to luxury; and regrettably, home and business care and repairs necessary for safety standards become something of an expendable concern while the industry revenue takes a sizable dip into the red.

Faced with a struggling economy and fewer and fewer clients, many architects I've met are asking themselves, "Why did I ever become an architect in the first place?"

And it isn't just a money problem. After 35 years of working with small businesses, many of them architectural firms, I'm convinced that the dissatisfaction experienced by countless architects is not just about money. To be frank, the recession doesn't deserve all the blame, either. While the financial crisis our country is facing certainly hasn't made things any better, the problem started long before the economy tanked. Let's dig a little deeper. Let's go back to school.

Can you remember that far back? Whichever university or college of architecture you attended, you probably had some great teachers who helped you become the fine architect you are. These schools excel at teaching the architecture; they'll teach you everything you need to know about computer graphic design, engineering, and public safety regulations and laws. But what they *don't* teach is the consummate skill set needed to be a successful architect, and they certainly don't teach what it takes to build a successful architectural firm.

Obviously, something is seriously wrong. The education that architects receive in school doesn't go far enough, deep enough, broad enough. Colleges of architecture don't teach you how to relate to the *enterprise* of architecture or to the *business* of architecture; they only teach you how to relate to the *practice* of architecture. In other words, they merely teach you how to be an *effective* rather than a *successful* architect. Last time I checked, they weren't offering degrees in success. That's why most architects are effective, but few are successful.

Although a successful architect must be effective, an effective architect does not have to be—and in most cases isn't—successful. An effective architect is capable of executing his or her duties with as much certainty and professionalism as possible.

A successful architect, on the other hand, works balanced hours, has little stress, leads rich and rewarding relationships with friends and family, and has an economic life that is diverse, fulfilling, and shows a continuous return on investment.

A successful architect finds time and ways to give back to the community but at little cost to his or her sense of ease.

A successful architect is a leader, not simply someone who teaches his clients how to understand constantly updated regulations, hazard laws, and how to protect the well-being of their home or business, but a sage; a rich person (in the broadest sense of the word); a strong father, mother, wife, or husband; a friend, teacher, mentor, and spiritually grounded human being; and a person who can see clearly into all aspects of what it means to lead a fulfilling life.

So let's go back to the original question. Why did you become an architect? Were you striving to just be an effective one, or did you dream about real and resounding success?

I don't know how you've answered that question in the past, but I am confident that once you understand the strategic thinking laid out in this book, you will answer it differently in the future. If the ideas here are going to be of value to you, it's critical that you begin to look at yourself in a different, more productive way. I am suggesting that you go beyond the mere technical aspects of your daily job as an architect and begin instead to think strategically about your architectural firm as both a business and an enterprise.

I often say that most *practices* don't work—the people who own them do. In other words, most architectural firms are jobs for the architects who own them. Does this sound familiar? The architect, overcome by an entrepreneurial seizure, has started his or her own firm, become his or her own boss, and now works for a lunatic!

The result: the architect is running out of time, patience, and ultimately money. Not to mention paying the worst price anyone can pay for the inability to understand what a true practice is, what a true business is, and what a true enterprise is—the price of his or her life.

In this book I'm going to make the case for why you should think differently about what you do and why you do it. It isn't just the future of your architectural firm that hangs in the balance. It's the future of your life.

The E-Myth Architect is an exciting departure from my other sole-authored books. In this book, an expert—a licensed architect who has successfully applied the E-Myth to the development of his architectural firm—is sharing his secrets about how he achieved extraordinary results using the E-Myth paradigm. In addition to the time-tested E-Myth strategies and systems I'll be sharing with you, you'll benefit from the wisdom, guidance, and practical tips provided by a legion of architects who've been in your shoes.

The problems that afflict architectural firms today don't only exist in the field of architecture; the same problems are confronting every organization of every size, in every industry in every country in the world. *The E-Myth Architect* is next in a new series of E-Myth Expert books that will serve as a launching pad for Michael E. Gerber Partners™ to bring a legacy of expertise to small, struggling businesses in all industries. This series will offer an exciting opportunity to understand and apply the significance of E-Myth methodology in both theory and practice to businesses in need of development and growth.

The E-Myth says that only by conducting your business in a truly innovative and independent way will you ever realize the unmatched joy that comes from creating a truly independent business, a business that works *without* you rather than *because* of you.

The E-Myth says that it is only by learning the difference between the work of a *business* and the business of *work* that architects will be freed from the predictable and often overwhelming tyranny of the unprofitable, unproductive routine that consumes them on a daily basis.

The E-Myth says that what will make the ultimate difference between the success or failure of your architectural firm is first and foremost how you *think* about your business, as opposed to how hard you work in it.

So, let's think it through together. Let's think about those things—work, clients, money, time—that dominate the world of architects everywhere.

Let's talk about planning. About growth. About management. About getting a life!

Let's think about improving your and your family's life through the development of an extraordinary practice. About getting the life you've always dreamed of but never thought you could actually have.

Envision the future you want, and the future is yours.

CHAPTER

1

The Story of Steve
and Peggy

Michael E. Gerber

*You leave home to seek your fortune and, when you get it, you go home
and share it with your family.*

—Anita Baker

very business is a family business. To ignore this truth is to
court disaster.

I don't care if family members actually work in the business or not. Whatever his or her relationship with the business, every member of an architect's family will be greatly affected by the decisions an architect makes about the business. There's just no way around it.

Unfortunately, like most businessmen, architects tend to compartmentalize their lives. They view their business as a profession—what they do—and therefore none of their family's business.

"This has nothing to do with you," says the architect to his wife, with blind conviction. "I leave work at the office and family at home." And with equal conviction, I say, "Not true!"

1

In actuality, your family and architect business are inextricably linked to one another. What's happening in your company is also happening at home. Consider if each of the following is true:

- If you're angry at work, you're also angry at home.
- If you're out of control at your architectural company, you're equally out of control at home.
- If you're having trouble with money in your company, you're also having trouble with money at home.
- If you have communication problems in your company, you're also having communication problems at home.
- If you don't trust in your company, you don't trust at home.
- If you're secretive in your company, you're equally secretive at home.

And you're paying a huge price for it!

The truth is that your company and your family are one—and you're the link. Or you should be. Because if you try to keep your company and your family apart, if your company and your family are strangers, you will effectively create two separate worlds that can never wholeheartedly serve each other. Two worlds that split each other apart.

Let me tell you the story of Steve and Peggy Walsh.

The Walshes met in college. They were lab partners in horticultural biology—Steve a student of architecture and Peggy in urban planning and design. When their lab discussions started to wander beyond building technology, theory of architecture and art, and environmental design into their personal lives, they discovered they had a lot in common. By the end of the course, they weren't just talking in class, they were talking on the phone every night—and not about architecture.

Steve thought Peggy was absolutely brilliant, and Peggy considered Steve the most passionate man she knew. It wasn't long before they were engaged and planning their future together. A week after graduation, they were married in a lovely garden ceremony outside Peggy's childhood home.

While Steve studied at a prestigious engineering, design, and architectural college, Peggy attended a prestigious land-based college nearby. Over the next few years, the couple worked hard to keep their finances afloat. They worked long hours and studied constantly; they were often exhausted and struggled to make ends meet. But throughout it all, they were committed to what they were doing and to each other.

After passing the Architecture Registration Exam (ARE), Steve went on to get a master's degree in architecture and environmental technologies, while Peggy completed her degree in urban design and planning. Then Steve started working for a large, multi-office architectural firm. Soon afterward, the couple had their first son, and Peggy decided to take some time off to be with him. Those were good years. Steve and Peggy loved each other very much, were active members in their church, participated in community organizations, and spent quality time together. The Walshes considered themselves one of the most fortunate families they knew.

But work became troublesome. Steve grew increasingly frustrated with the way the company was run. "I want to go into business for myself," he announced one night at the dinner table. "I want to start my own company."

Steve and Peggy spent many nights talking about the move. Was it something they could afford? Did Steve really have the skills necessary to make an architectural firm a success? Were there enough clients to go around? What impact would such a move have on Peggy's career managing a local plant nursery, their lifestyle, their son, their relationship? They asked all the questions they thought they needed to answer before Steve went into business for himself— but they never really drew up a concrete plan.

Finally, tired of talking and confident that he could handle whatever he might face, Steve committed to starting his own architecture and design company. Because she loved and supported him, Peggy agreed, offering her own commitment to help in any way she could. So Steve quit his job, took out a second mortgage on their home, and leased a small office nearby.

In the beginning, things went well. A building boom had hit the town, and new families were pouring into the area. Steve had no trouble getting new clients. His company expanded, quickly outgrowing his office.

Within a year, Steve had employed an office manager, Clarissa, to book appointments and handle the administrative side of the business. He also hired a bookkeeper, Tim, to handle the finances. Steve was ecstatic with the progress his young company had made. He celebrated by taking his wife and son on vacation to Italy.

Of course, managing a business was more complicated and time-consuming than working for someone else. Steve not only supervised all the jobs Clarissa and Tim did, he was continually looking for work to keep everyone busy. When he wasn't scanning journals of engineering and architecture to stay abreast of what was going on in the field or fulfilling continuing-education requirements to stay current on the latest standards of building codes, zoning laws, fire regulations, and other ordinances, he was going to the bank, wading through client paperwork, or speaking with building management companies. He also found himself spending more and more time on the telephone dealing with client complaints and nurturing relationships.

As the months went by and more and more clients came through the door, Steve had to spend even more time just trying to keep his head above water.

By the end of its second year, the company, now employing two full-time and two part-time people, had moved to a larger office downtown. The demands on Steve's time had grown with the company.

He began leaving home earlier in the morning, returning home later at night. He drank more. He rarely saw his son anymore. For the most part, Steve was resigned to the problem. He saw the hard work as essential to building the "sweat equity" he had long heard about.

Money was also becoming a problem for Steve. Although the company was growing like crazy, money always seemed scarce when it was really needed. He had discovered that commercial companies were often slow to pay. He had to go through anywhere from two to three people before he could find someone to speak with about non-payment of invoices that were thirty, sixty, or even ninety days out.

When Steve worked for somebody else, he was paid twice a month. In his own company, he often had to wait—sometimes for months. He was still owed money on billings he had completed more than ninety days before.

When he complained to late-paying commercial property management companies, it fell on deaf ears. They would shrug, smile, and promise to do their best, adding, "But you know how business is. The architectural industry has taken a huge hit and we're lucky if we can collect thirty- to forty-five days out!"

Of course, no matter how slowly Steve got paid, he still had to pay his people. This became a relentless problem. Steve often felt like a juggler dancing on a tightrope. A fire burned in his stomach day and night.

To make matters worse, Steve began to feel that Peggy was insensitive to his troubles. Not that he often talked to his wife about the company. "Business is business" was Steve's mantra. "It's my responsibility to handle things at the office and Peggy's responsibility to take care of her own job and the family."

Peggy herself was working late hours at her job, and they'd brought in a nanny to help with their son. Steve couldn't help but notice that his wife seemed resentful, and her apparent lack of understanding baffled him. Didn't she see that he had a company to take care of? That he was doing it all for his family? Apparently not.

As time went on, Steve became even more consumed and frustrated by his company. When he went off on his own, he remembered saying, "I don't like people telling me what to do." But people were still telling him what to do. On one particularly frustrating morning, his office had to spend forty-five minutes on hold, waiting to get detailed measurements of a conference room he was supposed to be working on that week. Steve was furious.

Not surprisingly, Peggy grew more frustrated by her husband's lack of communication. She cut back on her own hours at the nursery to focus on their family, but her husband still never seemed to be around. Their relationship grew tense and strained. The rare moments they were together were more often than not peppered by long silences—a far cry from the heartfelt conversations that had characterized their relationship's early days, when they'd talk into the wee hours of the morning.

Meanwhile, Tim, the bookkeeper, was also becoming a problem for Steve. Tim never seemed to have the financial information Steve needed to make decisions about payroll, client billing, and general operating expenses, let alone how much money was available for Steve and Peggy's living expenses.

When questioned, Tim would shift his gaze to his feet and say, "Listen, Steve, I've got a lot more to do around here than you can imagine. It'll take a little more time. Just don't press me, okay?"

Overwhelmed by his own work, Steve usually backed off. The last thing Steve wanted was to upset Tim and have to do the books himself. He could also empathize with what Tim was going through, given the company's growth over the past year.

Late at night in his office, Steve would sometimes recall his first years out of school. He missed the simple life he and his family had shared. Then, as quickly as the thoughts came, they would vanish. He had work to do and no time for daydreaming. "Having my own company is a great thing," he would remind himself. "I simply have to apply myself, as I did in school, and get on with the job. I have to work as hard as I always have when something needs to get done."

Steve began to live most of his life inside his head. He began to distrust his people. They never seemed to work hard enough or to care about his company as much as he did. If he wanted to get something done, he usually had to do it himself.

Then one day, the office manager, Clarissa, quit in a huff, frustrated by the amount of work her boss was demanding of her. Steve was left with a desk full of papers and a telephone that wouldn't stop ringing.

Clueless about the work Clarissa had done, Steve was overwhelmed by having to pick up the pieces of a job he didn't understand. His world turned upside down. He felt like a stranger in his own company.

Why had he been such a fool? Why hadn't he taken the time to learn what Clarissa did in the office? Why had he waited until now? Ever the trouper, Steve plowed into Clarissa's job with everything he could muster. What he found shocked him. Clarissa's workspace was a disaster area! Her desk drawers were a jumble of papers, coins, pens, pencils, rubber bands, envelopes, business cards, contact lenses, eye drops, and candy.

"What was she thinking?" Steve raged.

When he got home that night, even later than usual, he got into a shouting match with Peggy. He settled it by storming out of the house to get a drink. Didn't anybody understand him? Didn't anybody care what he was going through?

He returned home only when he was sure Peggy was asleep. He slept on the couch and left early in the morning, before anyone was awake. He was in no mood for questions or arguments.

When Steve got to his office the next morning, he immediately headed for the medicine cabinet. He had blisters on his hands, a backache, and a headache that just wouldn't quit! No matter how much pain he had physically, it was easier than having to deal with the mental anguish of his employee issues.

What lessons can we draw from Steve and Peggy's story? I've said it once and I'll say it again: Every business is a family business. Your business profoundly touches every member of your family, even if they never set foot inside your office. Every business either gives to the family or takes from the family, just as individual family members do.

If the business takes more than it gives, the family is always the first to pay the price. In order for Steve to free himself from the prison he created, he would first have to admit his vulnerability. He would have to confess to himself and his family that he really didn't know enough about his own company and how to grow it.

Steve tried to do it all himself. Had he succeeded, had the company supported his family in the style he imagined, he would have burst with pride. Instead, Steve unwittingly isolated himself, thereby achieving the exact opposite of what he sought.

He destroyed his life—and his family's life along with it.

Repeat after me: Every business is a family business.

Are you like Steve? I believe that all architects share a common soul with him. You must learn that a business is only a business. It is not your life. But it is also true that your business can have a profoundly negative impact on your life unless you learn how to do it differently than most other architects do it—and definitely differently than Steve did it.

Steve's architectural firm could have served his and his family's life. But for that to happen, he would have had to learn how to master his company in a way that was completely foreign to him.

Instead, Steve's company consumed him. Because he lacked a true understanding of the essential strategic thinking that would have allowed him to create something unique, Steve and his family were doomed from day one.

This book contains the secrets that Steve should have known. If you follow in Steve's footsteps, prepare to have your life and business fall apart. But if you apply the principles we'll discuss here, you can avoid a similar fate.

Let's start with the subject of money. But before we do, let's listen to the architect's view about the story I just told you. Let's talk about the story of Norbert's career—and yours. ✤

CHAPTER 2

The Love of Architecture

Norbert C. Lemermeyer

I hate intellectuals. They are from the top down. I am from the bottom up.
—Frank Lloyd Wright

May 11, 1976. That was the day I graduated from architecture school, and the day my future couldn't have felt more certain. I was about to embark on a career that would be creative and exciting, not to mention prestigious and well paying! Leave the tedious and humdrum work to someone else—I was going to be an *architect*.

At first, it was great. Better than great, really. It was everything I had hoped for and then some. I had a stable job, a good home life, and best of all, I was putting all those years of hard work at university to use, designing buildings and creating landmarks and making my mark on the world.

And then, reality started to set in.

It didn't take long for me to realize that I didn't want to spend the rest of my life working for someone else. I wanted to move upwards

9

and onwards, and the only way to do it was to start my own firm and carve out my own niche.

There was just one problem. Architecture school doesn't train you to run a business. We leave university knowing how to create beautiful structures and landmarks in cities. Businesses are proud to showcase our work; our own imaginations are the only limit to the myriad possibilities. When it comes to creating the structure of the business itself, we're stupefied.

Like other architects starting their own enterprise, I struggled to keep my head above water as I felt the challenges of running a business closing in on me. I had to attract and retain good, paying clients; I had to build solid working relationships with clients, contractors, and tradespeople; I had to stay on top of the leading and cutting-edge work going on in the field; I had to manage projects to ensure that the work was top-quality and that deadlines were met; I had to oversee all the staff needed to run the business; I had to maintain balance in my personal life.

Something had to give.

Amidst my efforts to hold it all together and make a decent go of running an architectural firm, my first marriage deteriorated. I spent long days (and sometimes nights) at the office, I took the stress of work home with me, and I became emotionally distant. I tried to convince myself it was the cost of greatness, a necessary sacrifice if I was ever to achieve my dream of running a successful architectural firm. In reality, it was just the first sign that I was doing it all wrong.

Unfortunately, my story is far from unique. Studies have shown that architects suffer from higher-than-normal rates of alcoholism, especially as they get older and the pressures of the job only get bigger. Architects have also been shown to suffer abnormally high rates of depression, and they more often experience divorce and family break-ups.

I've seen it happen. One architect friend of mine went into business, worked himself into the ground, and went bankrupt. He turned to drugs to help ease some of the pain, and in the process lost his wife and two beautiful children, eventually ending up living in his mother's basement. Worse still, I've seen colleagues commit suicide, all after going through the same experience of struggling to move from merely designing buildings to being practicing architects.

Most surprisingly of all, we architects seem to put up with all of this for surprisingly little money. The money becomes even less of an incentive when you realize that you're putting in 60, 80, sometimes even 100 hours a week only to find that you can't pay yourself until the client pays (and let's face it, sometimes they don't!), and you make sure your staff, bills, and fees are all paid first. We start to feel like failures, and the only thing that seems to make sense is to try to make up for a lack of business know-how with even more training or even more hours at the office. We tell concerned friends and family that it'll all be worth it in the end, but when is the end?

So that leads us to the real question at hand: How can we turn all of our hard work into tangible results, in enough time for us to actually enjoy the fruits of our labor?

We have all arrived at this place through different means, and we've all been led here by different goals and aspirations, but we share at least one thing in common. We're all struggling to turn our passions for architecture into solid, smooth-running businesses.

We're working long hours, we're taking work home, we're subjecting our families to our own stresses, and we're making compromise after compromise in the hopes that someday, it'll all pay off.

Worse yet, we're watching our dreams slip away. We're becoming bitter and jaded as our passions give way to doubt and, finally, regret. Architects trying to manage their own enterprises, large and small, are asking themselves, "Where did it all go wrong?"

The fact is, architects the world over set out on their own because they don't want to work for someone else, but in working for themselves, they end up, as Michael likes to say, "working for a lunatic." They don't recognize the self for whom they're working—and neither do their friends or families.

I know firsthand the pressures of running an architecture business, and I know how these pressures seep into your personal life, no matter how hard you try to leave them at the office. As an architect, I'm in charge of large sums of clients' monies, and each and every one of those clients wants to know that their money and time have been well spent. Each client's project is, to them, the most important matter in our office, and must be treated as such. One client may require their project to be started before winter sets in, another may want to review alternatives to the project, while another has seen something on the construction side that requires the architect's immediate attention. Add engineers, other consultants, contractors, strict building codes and bylaws, and unpredictable weather to the mix, and it's easy to see how priorities are always in a state of flux. And I, the architect, am in charge of all of it.

Every detail must be accounted for, and planning becomes the most important part of the job. Everything runs on a timeline, and putting something off until another day is out of the question. The results have to be amazing every time.

An architect's ability to do all of this successfully rests on their ability to manage their time and energy, but how can you manage your time when all your time is spent managing everything else?

When I first started my architecture business, most of my time was spent trying to get any and all business I could. Contracts coming through the door meant money, and money paid the bills and promised growth and success. Of course, more business meant more components to oversee. We hired more staff, all of whom had to be trained and then managed. Hiring more managers seemed like the logical solution, but they had to be managed, too. Then, of course, more staff on my payroll meant more pressure to get enough money coming in to pay them all on time!

In the end, my job was unrecognizable. I wasn't an architect. I wasn't using my years of hard work and training anymore. Most importantly, I wasn't exercising my passion. I was spending all of my energy doing everything I could to hold the business together, fearful of the new and unexpected problems that new business would surely bring, and I didn't have a clue what I was doing. Helpless doesn't even begin to describe what I was feeling.

It's taken a few decades and lots of experience talking to my colleagues who have gone through the same turmoil, but I've finally come out on the other side, and it's my mission to help you do the same. I know all too well how much time you stand to lose trying to figure it all out on your own, through trial and error, and I know how the stress quickly catches up with you, especially when it comes to your relationships and your mental and physical health.

Throughout this book I will refer to what my practice was like before I read *The E-Myth* and what my practice became after reading it. I will share with you my journey of applying Michael's E-Myth principles to an architectural practice, and I will give you firsthand insight into the intricacies of the field. I will describe how I went from a state of despondency to happiness, and how you can do the same.

So how did it happen? More importantly, how did I stop it from continuing? There is hope for you, just as there is for all smart business people who embrace the E-Myth way. Read on and discover how to take back your practice and your life, as I did. ✣

On the Subject
of Money

Michael E. Gerber

There are three faithful friends: an old wife, an old dog, and ready money.
—Benjamin Franklin

H ad Steve and Peggy first considered the subject of money as we will here, their lives could have been radically different.

Money is on the tip of every architect's tongue, on the edge (or at the very center) of every architect's thoughts, and intruding on every part of an architect's life.

Money is on the tip of every architect's tongue, on the edge (or at the very center) of every architect's thoughts, and intruding on every part of an architect's life.

With money consuming so much energy, why do so few architects handle it well? Why was Steve, like so many architects, willing to entrust his financial affairs to a relative stranger? Why is money scarce for most architects? Why is there less money than expected? And yet the demand for money is always greater than anticipated.

What is it about money that is so elusive, so complicated, so difficult to control? Why is it that every architect I've ever met hates to deal with the subject of money? Why are they almost always too late in facing money problems? And why are they constantly obsessed with the desire for more of it?

Money—you can't live with it and you can't live without it. But you better understand it and get your people to understand it. Because until you do, money problems will eat your business for lunch.

You don't need an accountant or financial planner to do this. You simply need to prod your people to relate to money very personally. From the architectural apprentice to receptionist, they should all understand the financial impact of what they do every day in relationship to the company's profit and loss.

And so you must teach your people to think like owners, not like technicians or office managers or receptionists. You must teach them to operate like personal profit centers, with a sense of how their work fits in with the company as a whole.

You must involve everyone in the company with the topic of money—how it works, where it goes, how much is left, and how much everybody gets at the end of the day. You also must teach them about the four kinds of money the company creates.

The Four Kinds of Money

In the context of owning, operating, developing, and exiting from an architectural firm, money can be split into four distinct but highly integrated categories:

- Income
- Profit
- Flow
- Equity

Failure to distinguish how the four kinds of money play out in your company is a surefire recipe for disaster.

Important Note: Do not talk to your accountants or book-keepers about what follows; it will only confuse them and you. This information comes from this real-life experiences of thousands of small-business owners, architects included, most of whom were hopelessly confused about money when I met them. Once they understood and accepted the following principles, they developed clarity about money that could only be called enlightenment.

The First Kind of Money: Income

Income is the money a company pays its architects for doing their job in the company. It's what they get paid for going to work every day.

Clearly, if architects didn't do their job, others would have to, and they would be paid the money the company currently pays the architects. Income, then, has nothing to do with *ownership*. Income is solely the province of employee-ship.

That's why to the architect-as-employee, income is the most important form money can take. To the architect-as-owner, however, it is the least important form money can take.

Most important; least important. Do you see the conflict between the architect-as-employee and the architect-as-owner?

We'll deal with this conflict later. For now, just know that it is potentially the most paralyzing conflict in an architect's life.

Failing to resolve this conflict will cripple you. Resolving it will set you free.

The Second Kind of Money: Profit

Profit is what's left over after an architectural firm has done its job effectively and efficiently. If there is no profit, the company is doing something wrong.

However, just because the company shows a profit does not mean it is necessarily doing all the right things in the right way. Instead, it just means that something was done right during or preceding the period in which the profit was earned.

The important issue here is whether the profit was intentional or accidental. If it happened by accident (which most profit does), don't take credit for it. You'll live to regret your impertinence.

If it happened intentionally, take all the credit you want. You've earned it. Because profit created intentionally, rather than by accident, is replicable—again and again. And your company's ability to repeat its performance is the most critical ability it can have.

As you'll soon see, the value of money is a function of your company's ability to produce it in predictable amounts at an above-average return on investment.

Profit can be understood only in the context of your company's purpose, as opposed to your purpose as an architect. Profit, then, fuels the forward motion of the company that produces it. This is accomplished in four ways:

- Profit is *investment capital* that feeds and supports growth.
- Profit is *bonus capital* that rewards people for exceptional work.
- Profit is *operating capital* that shores up money shortfalls.
- Profit is *return-on-investment capital* that rewards you, the owner-operator, for taking risks.

Without profit, an architectural firm cannot subsist, much less grow. Profit is the fuel of progress.

If a company misuses or abuses profit, however, the penalty is much like having no profit at all. Imagine the plight of an architect who has way too much return-on-investment capital and not enough investment capital, bonus capital, and operating capital. Can you see the imbalance this creates?

The Third Kind of Money: Flow

Flow is what money *does* in an architectural firm, as opposed to what money is. Whether the company is large or small, money tends to move erratically through it, much like a pinball. One minute it's there; the next minute it's not.

Flow can be even more critical to a company's survival than profit, because a company can produce a profit and still be short of money. Has this ever happened to you? It's called profit on paper rather than in fact.

No matter how large your company, if the money isn't there when it's needed, you're threatened—regardless of how much profit you've made. You can borrow it, of course. But money acquired in dire circumstances is almost always the most expensive kind of money you can get.

Knowing where the money is and where it will be when you need it is a critically important task for both the architect-as-employee and the architect-as-owner.

Rules of Flow

You will learn no more important lesson than the huge impact flow can have on the health and survival of your architecture practice, let alone your business or enterprise. The following two rules will help you understand why this subject is so critical.

1. The First Rule of Flow states that your income statement is static, while the flow is dynamic. Your income statement is a snapshot, while the flow is a moving picture. So, while your income statement is an excellent tool for analyzing your practice *after* the fact, it's a poor tool for managing it in the heat of the moment.

Your income statement tells you (1) how much money you're spending and where, and (2) how much money you're receiving and from where.

Flow gives you the same information as the income statement; plus, it tells you when you're spending and receiving money. In other words, flow is an income statement moving through time. And that is the key to understanding flow. It is about management in real time. How much is coming in? How much is going out? You'd like to know this daily, or even by the hour if possible. Never by the week or month.

You must be able to forecast flow. You must have a flow plan that helps you gain a clear vision of the money that's out there next month and the month after that. You must also pinpoint what your needs will be in the future.

Ultimately, however, when it comes to flow, the action is always in the moment. It's about now. The minute you start to meander away from the present, you'll miss the boat.

Unfortunately, few architects pay any attention to flow until it dries up completely and slow pay becomes no pay. They are oblivious to this kind of detail until, say, clients announce that they won't pay for this or that. That gets an architect's attention because the expenses keep on coming.

When it comes to flow, most architects are flying by the proverbial seat of their pants. No matter how many people you hire to take care of your money, until you change the way you think about it, you will always be out of luck. No one can do this for you.

Managing flow takes attention to detail. But when flow is managed, your life takes on an incredible sheen. You're swimming with the current, not against it. You're in charge!

2. The Second Rule of Flow states that money seldom moves as you expect it to. But you do have the power to change that, provided you understand the two primary sources of money as it comes in and goes out of your architect business.

The truth is, the more control you have over the source of money, the more control you have over its flow. The sources of money are both inside and outside your company.

Money comes from *outside* your company in the form of receivables, reimbursements, investments, and loans.

Money comes from *inside* your company in the form of payables, taxes, capital investments, and payroll. These are the costs associated with attracting clients, delivering your services, handling operations, and so forth.

Few architects see the money going out of their company as a source of money, but it is.

When considering how to spend money in your business, you can save—and therefore make—money in three ways:

- Do it more effectively.
- Do it more efficiently.
- Stop doing it altogether.

By identifying the money sources inside and outside of your company, and then applying these methods, you will be immeasurably better at controlling the flow in your company.

But what are these sources? They include how you

- manage your services;
- buy supplies and equipment;
- compensate your people;
- plan people's use of time;
- determine the direct cost of your services;
- increase the number of clients seen;
- manage your work;
- collect account receivables; and
- countless more.

In fact, every task performed in your company (and ones you haven't yet learned how to perform) can be done more efficiently and effectively, dramatically reducing the cost of doing business. In the process, you will create more income, produce more profit, and balance the flow.

The Fourth Kind of Money: Equity

Sadly, few architects fully appreciate the value of equity in their architectural firm. Yet equity is the second most valuable asset any will ever possess. (The first most valuable asset is, of course, your life. More on that later.)

Equity is the financial value a prospective buyer places on your company.

Thus, your company is your most important product, not your services, because your company has the power to set you free. That's right. Once you sell your company—providing you get what you want for it—you're free!

Of course, to enhance your equity—to increase your value—you have to build it right. You have to build a company that works. A company that can become a true business, and a business that can become a true enterprise. A company/business/enterprise that can produce income, profit, flow, and equity better than any other architect's company—or practice—can.

To accomplish that, your company must be designed so it can do what it does systematically and predictably, every single time.

The Story of McDonald's

Let me tell you what is probably the most unlikely story anyone has ever told you about the successful building of a company, business, and enterprise. Let me tell you the story of Ray Kroc.

You might be thinking, *What on earth does a hamburger stand have to do with my company? I'm not in the hamburger business; I'm an architect.*

Yes, you are. But by practicing architecture as you have been taught, you've abandoned any chance to expand your reach, help more clients, or improve your services the way they must be improved if the business of architecture—and your life—is going to be transformed.

The answer lies in Ray Kroc's story.

Kroc called his first McDonald's restaurant "a little money machine." That's why thousands of franchises bought it. And the reason it worked? Kroc demanded consistency, so that a hamburger in Philadelphia would be an advertisement for one in Peoria. In fact, no matter where you bought a McDonald's hamburger in the 1950s, the meat patty was guaranteed to weigh exactly 1.6 ounces, with a diameter of 3⅝ inches. It was in the McDonald's handbook.

Did Kroc succeed? You know he did! And so can you, once you understand his methods. Consider just one part of his story.

In 1954, Kroc made his living selling the five-spindle Multimixer milkshake machine. He heard about a hamburger stand in San Bernardino, California, that had eight of his machines in operation, meaning it could make forty shakes simultaneously. This he had to see. Kroc flew from Chicago to Los Angeles, then drove sixty miles to San Bernardino. As he sat in his car outside Mac and Dick McDonald's restaurant, he watched as lunch customers lined up for bags of hamburgers.

In a revealing moment, Kroc approached a strawberry blonde in a yellow convertible. As he later described it, "It was not her sex appeal but the obvious relish with which she devoured the hamburger that made my pulse begin to hammer with excitement."

Passion.

In fact, it was the French fry that truly captured his heart. Before the 1950s, it was almost impossible to buy fries of consistent quality. Kroc changed all that. "The French fry," he once wrote, "would become almost sacrosanct for me, its preparation a ritual to be followed religiously."

Passion and preparation.

The potatoes had to be just so—top-quality Idaho russets, eight ounces apiece, deep-fried to a golden brown, and salted with a shaker that, as Kroc put it, kept going "like a Salvation Army girl's tambourine."

As Kroc soon learned, potatoes too high in water content—even top-quality Idaho russets varied greatly in water content—will come out soggy when fried. And so Kroc sent out teams of workers, armed with hydrometers, to make sure all his suppliers were producing potatoes in the optimal solids range of 20 to 23 percent.

Preparation and passion. Passion and preparation. Look those words up in the dictionary and you'll see Kroc's picture. Can you envision your picture there?

Do you understand what Kroc did? Do you see why he was able to sell thousands of franchises? Kroc knew the true value of equity, and, unlike Steve from our story, Kroc went to work *on* his business rather than *in* his business. He knew the hamburger wasn't his product—McDonald's was!

So what does *your* architectural firm need to do to become a little money machine? What is the passion that will drive you to build a company that works—a turnkey system like Ray Kroc's?

Equity and the Turnkey System

What's a turnkey system? And why is it so valuable to you? To better understand it, let's look at another example of a turnkey system that worked to perfection: the recordings of Frank Sinatra.

Sinatra's records were to him as McDonald's restaurants were to Ray Kroc. They were part of a turnkey system that allowed Sinatra to sing to millions of people without having to be present.

Sinatra's recordings were a dependable turnkey system that worked predictably, systematically, automatically, and effortlessly to produce the same results every single time—no matter where they were played, and no matter who was listening.

Regardless of where Sinatra was, his records just kept on producing income, profit, flow, and equity, over and over—and still do! Sinatra needed only to produce the prototype recording and the system did the rest.

Kroc's McDonald's is another prototypical turnkey solution, addressing everything McDonald's needs to do in a basic, systematic way so that anyone properly trained by McDonald's can successfully reproduce the same results.

And this is where you'll realize your equity opportunity: in the way your company does business; in the way your company systematically does what you intend it to do; and in the development of your turnkey system—a system that works even in the hands of ordinary people (and architects less experienced than you) to produce extraordinary results.

Remember:

- If you want to build vast equity in your company, then go to work *on* your company, building it into a business that works every single time.

- Go to work *on* your company to build a totally integrated turnkey system that delivers exactly what you promised every single time.

- Go to work *on* your company to package it and make it stand out from the other architectural firms you see everywhere else.

Here is the most important idea you will ever hear about your company and what it can potentially provide for you:

The value of your equity is directly proportional to how well your company works. And how well your company works is directly proportional to the effectiveness of the systems you have put into place upon which the operation of your company depends.

Whether money takes the form of income, profit, flow, or equity, the amount of it—and how much of it stays with you—invariably boils down to this. Money, happiness, life—it all depends on how well your company works. Not on your people, not on you, but on the system.

Your company holds the secret to more money. Are you ready to learn how to find it?

Earlier in this chapter, I alerted you to the inevitable conflict between the architect-as-employee and the architect-as-owner. It's a battle between the part of you working *in* the company and the part of you working *on* the company. Between the part of you working for income and the part of you working for equity.

Here's how to resolve this conflict:

- Be honest with yourself about whether you're filling *employee* shoes or *owner* shoes.

- As your company's key employee, determine the most effective way to do the job you're doing, *and then document that job.*

- Once you've documented the job, create a strategy for replacing yourself with someone else (another architect, or, even better, a technician) who will then use your documented system exactly as you do.

- Have your new employees manage the newly delegated system. Improve the system by quantifying its effectiveness over time.

- Repeat this process throughout your company wherever you catch yourself acting as employee rather than owner.

- Learn to distinguish between ownership work and employee-ship work every step of the way.

Master these methods, understand the difference between the four kinds of money, develop an interest in how money works in your company—and then watch it flow in with the speed and efficiency of an avalanche.

Now let's take another step in our strategic thinking process. Let's look at the subject of *planning*. But first, let's listen to what Norbert has to say about money. ✤

Money in Perspective

Norbert C. Lemermeyer

The difference between failure & success is doing a thing nearly right and doing it exactly right.

—Edward Simmons

What is it about money that drives us to insanity?

Somewhere along the way, I got the notion that money was the key to happiness. Although publicly I might deny that I live by such an absurd and shallow concept, my actions say otherwise.

Every day, I meet seemingly educated and intelligent people, who still behave as if their happiness level is directly tied to the number of zeros in their bank account. Ironically, the harder and longer they work, the less they seem to have of either money *or* happiness. But rather than stop the insanity and try a new approach, these intelligent, educated people find ways to devote more hours to the alchemic art of turning money into happiness.

So, does this mean that you have to choose between being happy and making some real dough? Are you struggling, thinking that you can't have both? Absolutely not! In fact, I'm all for prosperity and "living the good life," and I applaud the determination to create a comfortable and financially secure existence for you and yours.

It's not the dream that I question here; it's the approach that needs some work, and if there's one thing you take away from this book, let it be this: Money alone will not give you the life you're looking for—only you can do that. What's more, to get to that life you're seeking, you have to give up the idea that you are what you do.

The most difficult perspective I've had to grasp is that a business practice is separate from myself. The notion that I am forever destined to trade my time for dollars was deeply, and hopelessly, ingrained in me. I shared the conviction of most architects—that getting more projects and working longer hours would make all the money problems go away.

What I failed to realize is that even if I did generate more cash flow, I was sacrificing something worth far more—myself. That isn't a recipe for success, but rather one that guarantees burnout and disaster. Just ask me.

A huge breakthrough occurred when I realized I could create a business that would leverage my time and the revenue of the firm. However, this new awareness of "architect as entrepreneur" had to be reinforced often so that I didn't inevitably slip back into the "architect as employee" mindset.

Remember, the underlying purpose of this book is for you to take stock of your practice and be honest about the work you do. Just as Ray Kroc realized that his product wasn't hamburgers, but rather, the business that made the hamburgers, all architects who come to think of the architectural practice itself as the real product of their efforts are on their way to a better, more rewarding life.

Once I began to see my practice as a separate thing that I could mold, tinker with, and redesign any way I wanted, it was just like when I, as an architect, looked at the model of a building I planned to build. I stepped back and saw the parts of my architectural practice as components that could be optimized and systematized. Can you do that?

If not, then all the strategies Michael E. Gerber and I are going to lay out in this book will make no sense. However, once you grasp the fundamental distinction between your work as an employee and your responsibilities as an owner, you have entered the exciting world of being the designer, builder, and creator of your business life.

The skills of a business owner are not the same as those of a first-class designer/architect. Just because you're a great designer/architect, doesn't mean you know what it takes to run a business that provides architectural services. Competency in business doesn't come naturally, and if these concepts are new, you really can't be blamed. Architectural schools, traditionally, have not focused on the business of architecture. They are in the technician business, teaching students how to think like architects and solve architectural problems.

Some progressive schools of architecture have begun to address this obvious shortcoming in the typical architectural school curriculum. However, the attitude prevailing in the schools of architecture, that business is of lesser importance, does little for practicing architects slugging it out in the trenches, trying to meet payroll and create better lives for their families. If you're willing to suspend all your beliefs about what it takes to build a successful architectural firm, this book will give you a new track to run on. It will be a chance to reorganize your thoughts and right your ship before it sinks.

Once I was clear about my vision of my architectural firm as a business, I committed it to writing and passionately communicated it to everyone in the practice, from the receptionist, to the technicians, to the bookkeeper, to the other architects and even to my family, as I hoped to get support for this new way of serving clients and earning a living. Clear, effective communication with my staff was critical in my new venture. Because my business was run in large part by employees, it was imperative they all understand the big picture. The big picture was about money, finances, profitability, paychecks and bonuses—yes, bonuses!

I recommend that the first step is know your target numbers and write them down as annual revenue and expenses. Revenue minus expenses equals the income you target for your use as owner. These numbers are divided into 12 parts so you can monitor your monthly numbers and act upon them. You can further break down your numbers into weekly targets. These monthly/weekly numbers make your annual target numbers a reality that you can closely follow. When you review your numbers weekly, you know whether you have achieved your targets or not. These numbers are shared with the team, and everyone in the firm can see the results of their efforts. The target numbers form a single-minded goal for your entire team.

Once your team buys into this, the possibilities are endless. Celebrations can be arranged weekly, monthly, or quarterly for meeting the goals. The team members know that bonuses are dependent on exceeding those target numbers. It's no longer a mystery how money is distributed. Once you frame your numbers properly and keep your team apprised of them, everyone will jump on board.

Production targets will be met. Client fees will be easily collected. Vendors will have bills thoroughly scrutinized. Requests for frivolous expenditures will stop, and each employee will start paying attention to the productivity of other staff members. If some slack off, others will be there to remind them that they're messing with the bonuses. This system works magic in my office, especially when compared to the early years, when I kept the numbers tight to my chest.

Understanding *flow* requires that you actually analyze the ebb and flow of money through your practice. Depending on your type of practice, you may have noticed that it has a rhythm of its own. There are wild fluctuations in revenue and expenses in an architectural firm. Architects billing on a hourly basis see more predictable patterns. Whatever the variations, you need a strategy to ensure that there are always funds available.

An adequate line of credit (LOC) is necessary to withstand the flow variances and smooth out the accounts receivable from the accounts payable, whether you think you need it or not. It can have a devastating impact on architectural practices when credit is not available. The best time to ask for an LOC is when the money is not needed. That's when banks are most likely to say yes because it's low-risk business for them.

Regardless of whether you're starting a practice or enhancing your current business, now is the time to get your "unnecessary" LOC.

I recommend that you establish at least one solid relationship with a local banker. This personal relationship makes all the difference. Take the time to seek one out and candidly explain the kind of practice you have and your credit needs. In tough times, it will be that person who takes up your cause to the nameless committees that make the decisions.

Trusted bankers sometimes move from institution to institution as they seek to advance their careers. I recommend that you move with them. In shaky times, credit lifelines may mean the difference between prosperity and bankruptcy, so don't overlook the importance of these relationships.

In addition to a banker connection, a strong bond with a certified accountant (CPA) or experienced bookkeeper is required. Many small architectural firms and solo practitioners try to skimp on this relationship. Some architects run their practices out of their checkbooks and a personal copy of Quicken. Commitment to having a real business means you'll need to have instant control and access to your numbers. Your numbers tell a story about your firm. It's unbiased, unsentimental, and devoid of wishful thinking. Every architectural firm needs a strong relationship with an accountant, who knows your numbers and can interpret them for you.

Before the fifteenth day of every month, my bookkeeper provides me with a management report, which provides a detailed account of all the financial information that is required to run the business. With this information, any adjustments required to keep the business on track can be made with the latest financial records—the truth about the previous month. With this report I can focus on the financial health of the business to make sure it's profitable and has liquidity. I also can see if equity in the business is accumulating. The monthly income statement and balance sheet point out any patterns, good or bad. It's also a chance to review your expenses to make sure they're in check.

To zero in on particular numbers, the accountant can use various benchmarks or ratios to judge the health of your practice. Over the years, I've created several that help point out the critical metrics. The ratios may be different among different types of practices, but taking the time to identify those numbers will pay huge dividends down the road. If a particular month shows that these ratios are out of whack, red flags go up and I can take corrective action.

Revenue Canada, the Canadian counterpart of the U.S. Internal Revenue Service, has taken national surveys to help you sort out some often-used ratios for various part of your business. Common size ratios, for example, express each category from your balance sheet as a percentage of your total assets and liabilities. You can do the same with the income statement and calculate the percentage each income item represents of your total sales. Your current ratio divides your current assets by your current liabilities to show the financial health of your enterprise.

What will all these ratios do for you? Wouldn't it be helpful to know what percentage of your revenue should be devoted to marketing or rent or salaries? Would you like to know the cost of a client acquisition? How about a healthy ratio for owner's compensation? Without calculating these numbers on a monthly basis, you're flying blind.

Most architects don't think about equity because they don't think about their architectural practice as a business. Consequently, they never consider the natural conclusion of an enterprise, that is, the profitable exit or the sale of the practice. Most architects never consider the sale of the firm. The primary value of your practice is in your systems, and those can be sold for a handsome sum. The very essence of a business will be a pot of money down the road when it's time for you to go.

Take the time to examine the "money issues" in your practice and see how you stack up against the four factors. Then envision how you could take all four money factors into account as you go forward in your practice. The gap between the way you used to think about money and how you now think of money will be closed as we move forward and begin the planning process. ❧

On the Subject of Planning

Michael E. Gerber

Luck is good planning, carefully executed.

—Anonymous

Another obvious oversight revealed in Steve and Peggy's story was the absence of true planning.

An architect lacking a plan is simply someone who goes to work every day. Someone who is just doing it, doing it, doing it. Busy, busy, busy. Maybe making money, maybe not. Maybe getting something out of life, maybe not. Taking chances without really taking control.

The plan tells anyone who needs to know how we do things here. The plan defines the objective and the process by which you will attain it. The plan encourages you to organize tasks into functions, and then helps people grasp the logic of each of those functions. This in turn permits you to bring new employees up to speed quickly.

There are numerous books and seminars on the subject of business management, but they focus on making you a better architect. I want to teach you something that you've never been taught before: how to be a manager. It has nothing to do with conventional business management and everything to do with thinking like an entrepreneur.

The Planning Triangle

As we discussed in the preface, every architect sole proprietorship is a company, every architect business is a company, and every architect enterprise is a company. Yet the difference between the three is extraordinary. Although all three may offer architectural services, how they do what they do is completely different.

The trouble with most architectural companies owned by an architect is they are dependent on the architect. That's because they're sole proprietorships—the smallest, most limited form a company can take. Sole proprietorships are formed around the technician, whether architect or roofer.

You may choose in the beginning to form a sole proprietorship, but you should understand its limitations. The company called a *sole proprietorship* depends on the owner—that is, the architect. The company called a *business* depends on other people plus a system by which that business does what it does. Once your sole proprietorship becomes a business, you can replicate it, turning it into an *enterprise*.

Consider the example of Sea Home Architecture. The clients don't come in asking for Douglas Sea, although he is one of the top architects around. After all, he can only handle so many projects a day and be in only one location at a time.

Yet, he wants to offer his high-quality services to more people in the community. If he has reliable systems in place—systems that any qualified subcontractor can learn to use—he has created a business and it can be replicated. Douglas can then go on to offer his services—which demand his guidance, not his presence—in a multitude of different settings. He can open dozens of architectural firms, none of which needs Douglas Sea himself, except in the role of entrepreneur.

Is your architectural firm going to be a sole proprietorship, a business, or an enterprise? Planning is crucial to answering this all-important question. Whatever you choose to do must be communicated by your plan, which is really three interrelated plans in one. We call it the Planning Triangle, and it consists of

- the business plan;
- the job plan; and
- the completion plan.

The three plans form a triangle, with the business plan at the base, the job plan in the center, and the completion plan at the apex.

The business plan determines who you are (the business), the job plan determines what you do (the specific focus of your architectural business), and the completion plan determines how you do it (the fulfillment process).

By looking at the Planning Triangle, we see that the three critical plans are interconnected. The connection between them is established by asking the following questions:

1. Who are we?
2. What do we do?
3. How do we do it?

Who are we? is purely a strategic question.
What do we do? is both a strategic and a tactical question.
How do we do it? is both a strategic and a tactical question.

Strategic questions shape the vision and destiny of your business, of which your practice is only one essential component. Tactical questions turn that vision into reality. Thus, strategic questions provide the foundation for tactical questions, just as the base provides the foundation for the middle and apex of your Planning Triangle.

First ask: What do we do and how do we do it ... *strategically?*
And then: What do we do and how do we do it ... *practically?*
Let's look at how the three plans will help you develop your practice..

The Business Plan

Your business plan will determine what you choose to do in your architectural business and the way you choose to do it. Without a business plan, your business can do little more than survive. And even that will take more than a little luck.

Without a business plan, you're treading water in a deep pool with no shore in sight. You're working against the natural flow.

I'm not talking about the traditional business plan taught in business schools. No, this business plan reads like a story—the most important story you will ever tell.

Your business plan must clearly describe

- the business you are creating;
- the purpose it will serve;

- the vision it will pursue;
- the process through which you will turn that vision into a reality; and
- the way money will be used to realize your vision.

Build your business plan with business language, not practice language (the architect's language). Make sure the plan focuses on matters of interest to your lenders and shareholders rather than just your technicians. It should rely on demographics and psychographics to tell you who buys and why; it should also include projections for return on investment and return on equity. Use it to detail both the market and the strategy through which you intend to become a leader in that market, not as an architect but as a business enterprise.

The business plan, though absolutely essential, is only one of three critical plans every architect needs to create and implement. Now let's take a look at the job plan.

The Job Plan

The job plan includes everything an architect needs to know, have, and do to deliver his or her promise to a client on time, every time.

Every task should prompt you to ask three questions:

1. What do I need to know?
2. What do I need to have?
3. What do I need to do?

What Do I Need to Know?

What information do I need to satisfy my promise on time, every time, exactly as promised? To recognize what you need to know, you must understand the expectations and limitations of others, including your clients, administrators, managers, architects, subcontractors, designers, and other employees. Are you clear on those expectations? Don't make the mistake of assuming you know. Instead, create a need-to-know checklist to make sure you ask all the necessary questions.

A need-to-know checklist might look like this:

- What are my clients' expectations?
- What are my subcontractors' expectations?
- What are my staff's expectations?
- What are my vendors' expectations?

What Do I Need to Have?

This question raises the issue of resources—namely, money, people, and time. If you don't have enough money to finance operations, how can you fulfill those expectations without creating cash-flow problems? If you don't have a sufficient number of people or people with sufficient skills, what happens then? And if you don't have enough time to manage the job to completion, what happens when you can't be in two places at once?

Again, don't assume that you can get what you need when you need it. Most often, you can't. And even if you can get what you need at the last minute, you'll pay dearly for it.

What Do I Need to Do?

The focus here is on actions to be started and finished. *What do I need to do to fulfill the expectations of this client on time, every time, exactly as promised?* For example, what exactly is necessary to build a segmental retaining wall, install a paver patio, or install a design plan?

Your clients fall into distinct categories, and those categories make up your business. The best architectural firms will invariably focus on fewer and fewer categories as they discover the importance of doing one thing better than anyone else. Answering the question *What do I need to do?* demands a series of action plans, including

- the objective to be achieved;
- the standards by which you will know that the objective has been achieved;
- the benchmarks you need to reach for the objective to be achieved;
- the function/person accountable for the completion of the benchmarks;
- the budget for the completion of each benchmark; and
- the time by which each benchmark must be completed.

Your action plans should become the foundation for the completion plans. The reason you need completion plans is to ensure that everything you do is not only realistic but can also be managed.

The Completion Plan

If the job plan gives you results and provides you with standards, the completion plan tells you everything you need to know about every benchmark in the job plan—that is, how you're going to fulfill client expectations on time, every time, as promised. In other words, how you're going to install an HVAC system and educate a client on proper operations.

The completion plan is essentially the operations manual, providing information about the details of doing tactical work. It is a guide to tell the people responsible for doing that work exactly how to do it.

Every completion plan becomes a part of the knowledge base of your business. No completion plan goes to waste. Every completion plan becomes a kind of textbook that explains to new employees or new subcontractors joining your team how your business operates in a way that distinguishes it from all other architectural firms.

To return to an earlier example, the completion plan for making a Big Mac is explicitly described in the *McDonald's Operation Manual*, as is every completion plan needed to run a McDonald's business.

The completion plan for an architect might include the step-by-step details of how to lay out a conference room based on a scaled drawing or how to organize the supplies for the job to minimize movement of materials or the sequence of steps that create a successful architecture business. Of course, all those who work in architecture have to watch what their competitors are doing. They've learned to do it the same way everyone else has learned to do it. But if you are going to stand out as unique in the minds of your clients, employees, and others, you must invent your own way of doing even ordinary things. Most of that value-added perception will come from your communication skills, your listening skills, and your innovative skills in transforming an ordinary visit into a great, value-added client experience.

Perhaps you'll decide that a mandatory part of the "as-built" plan will be identifying the fire codes for installation and explaining what the different codes mean so clients have a better understanding of the routing of their building plan. If no other architect your clients have seen has ever taken the time to explain the procedure, you'll immediately set yourself apart. You must constantly raise the questions: How do we do it here? How should we do it here?

The quality of your answers will determine how effectively you distinguish your business from every other architect's business.

Benchmarks

You can measure the movement of your business—from what it is today to what it will be in the future—using business benchmarks. These are the goals you want your business to achieve during its lifetime.

Your benchmarks should include the following:

- Financial benchmarks
- Emotional benchmarks (the impact your company will have on everyone who comes into contact with it)
- Performance benchmarks
- Client benchmarks (Who are they? Why do they come to you? What will your company give them that no one else will?)
- Employee benchmarks (How do you grow people? How do you find people who want to grow? How do you create a school in your company that will teach your people skills they can't learn anywhere else?)

Your business benchmarks will reflect (1) the position your company will hold in the minds and hearts of your clients, employees, and investors, and (2) how you intend to make that position a reality through the systems you develop.

Your benchmarks will describe how your management team will take shape and what systems you will need to develop so your managers, just like McDonald's managers, will be able to produce the results for which they will be held accountable.

Benefits of the Planning Triangle

By implementing the Planning Triangle, you will discover:

- what your company will look, act, and feel like when it's fully evolved;
- when that's going to happen;
- how much money you will make; and
- much more.

These, then, are the primary purposes of the three critical plans: (1) to clarify precisely what needs to be done to get what the architect wants from his or her company and life, and (2) to define the specific steps by which it will happen.

First *this* must happen, then *that* must happen. One, two, three. By monitoring your progress, step by step, you can determine whether you're on the right track.

That's what planning is all about. It's about creating a standard—a yardstick—against which you will be able to measure your performance.

Failing to create such a standard is like throwing a straw into a hurricane. Who knows where that straw will land?

Have you taken the leap? Have you accepted that the words *business* and *practice* are not synonymous? That a sole proprietorship relies on the architect and a business relies on other people plus a system?

Because most architects are control freaks, 99 percent of today's architectural companies are sole proprietorships, not businesses.

The result, as a friend of mine says, is that "architects are spending all day stamping out fires when all around them the forest is ablaze. They're out of touch, and that architect better take control of the business before someone else does."

Because architects are never taught to think like entrepreneurs, the architect professional is forever at war with the entrepreneur. This is especially evident in large, multi-location companies, where there is no personal relationship with the owner, where bureaucrats (corporate management) often try to control architects (entrepreneurs). They usually end up treating each other as combatants. In fact, the single greatest reason architects become entrepreneurs is to divorce such bureaucrats and to begin to reinvent the architect enterprise.

That's you. Now the divorce is over and a new love affair has begun. You're an architect with a plan! Who wouldn't want to do business with such a person?

To find a template of what your three critical plans may look like when they're finished, go to www.michaelegerber.com/co-author.

Now let's take the next step in our strategic odyssey and take a closer look at the subject of management. But before we do, read what Norbert has to say on the subject of planning. ❦

CHAPTER

6

Not Without Planning

Norbert C. Lemermeyer

When a man does not know what harbor he is making for, no wind is the right wind.

— Seneca

Now that you've read Michael's chapter on planning, you should feel excited about this new perspective and the opportunities it brings. And yet, you're probably thinking, "Planning? When do I have time to plan? I'm already working nearly every waking hour!"

Chapter 5 is essentially a blueprint to transform your "practice" into a "business," and if you follow it, I assure you results. It works so well, in fact, that I used it and continue to use it on my own business. I have experienced a complete transformation, from being a business scrambling from crisis to crisis, to one where management systems are in place to handle all aspects of the business in a professional manner in the normal course of providing services. All team members know

43

exactly what to do and what to expect from their team members while giving high level service to clients.

The following is how this transformation will take place. It is important to highlight certain components of the planning process as well as add some key elements specifically for the architect. So I'll start with a baseline developed from firsthand experience.

This is where I was. I have always done superior architectural work, but the practice did not mature into a profitable business, and I felt frustrated and helpless to make my dreams come true. I was convinced that my daily schedule did not permit the time to think about "working on the business," because I had too many more urgent matters waiting on my desk every day.

Clients, meetings, troubleshooting on projects, and busywork were just a few of the things that kept me from the all-important activity of strategic planning. Of course, let's not forget, my need to stay on top of my projects, keep the documents I used in my practice up to date, monitor new products and code changes, and make sure my architectural firm was equipped with the latest technology. Have I missed anything?

I was expected to do all of this while making sure that I paid attention to staff, provided training when they needed it, and scheduled performance reviews in a timely manner. This long list of responsibilities caused me to look at planning as a sort of academic exercise for those with nothing to do.

At the same time, I had to get back to work. Unfortunately, that meant busywork, the "doing it, doing it, doing it" all day long, into the night and on weekends as well.

In reality, ignoring the time to "sharpen the saw" and critically look at my practice as a business was the one thing that prevented me from developing a predictably profitable enterprise.

I've found that regardless of how many pressing matters might be demanding my attention, real-world planning must be the engine that guides all of my business decisions. The most important part of my day, my week, my month, and each and every year, is committing to my vision of writing it and then mapping out the steps to make it happen. This is no an easy task, and it may go against the natural instinct to jump in and get things done, but the transformation began when I started to set aside time for this strategic activity.

As Michael E. Gerber pointed out many years ago in his landmark book, *The E-Myth*, the primary purpose of my business is to serve my needs—to be a vehicle for my happiness and fulfillment. Unfortunately, this first principle has been turned on its head. Not long after I was a new architect, getting into the groove of practicing, something amazing happened: The practice started running me instead. As Emerson once wisely said, "Things are in the saddle and ride mankind." In my case and in the cases of far too many of my colleagues, the practice has become the master and the owner is only along for the ride.

That's why I like the triangle structure in Chapter 5 so much. This is a perfect model for architects, regardless of their practice area. I set aside a couple of days of focused time to think about how it could work in my firm. Simply asking, "Who am I? What do I do? How do I do it?" can often be all it takes to open the channels to a new way of thinking. Before reading about the E-Myth, these fundamental questions had never been asked because the technician in me just jumped in and started practicing. This book became my "time-out" from all the frantic activity. It was the savior of not only my business, but my career in architecture. It has the potential to save you, too, if you make the time to follow these recommendations and put them to use. Reading the words and understanding the concepts are not enough. Action must be taken to see the rewards.

Your Business Plan

The plan should not be a dry academic piece, but a rich story about the business you've brought into existence. It's something much more than a means to put bread on the table. It has a purpose in the community and will impact employees, consultants, vendors, and, of course, clients. The business plan will be the firm's constitution, outlining the vision and how you plan to bring it into reality.

To get started, calendar some time for a personal retreat to really explore the practice, its purpose, and how it fits with your original intention. The first exercise should be to honestly look at the specific area of architecture in which you are practicing, or in some cases, where you want to practice. This is a core issue because many architects would rather practice in another area. They got into their specific area in a variety of ways, none of which had anything to do with what they really wanted out of their architectural career. Perhaps they got a job with a firm where a project architect was needed and they became a project architect. Others got involved in design, no doubt attracted by the glamour and excitement of design work, only to find a life filled with long hours and stress, occasionally punctuated by an actual, challenging design project.

Despite how you got there, practicing in an area where there is no passion or joy is a recipe for unhappiness, regardless of the money made. So, set aside all those reasons and circumstances that have brought you to this point. Put all the cards on the table and invent the life you want. It's never too late, and who knows? You may fall in love with your practice choice all over again.

It may take some soul searching to come to grips with feelings about your current practice area, but don't underestimate the importance of this journey. To be fulfilled, you need a burning desire to go to work each day and build the practice. If that is not how you feel, you need to reconsider what you are doing. There is a wide field of opportunity within architecture. Many architects have a romantic idea of how architecture might be practiced. This mindset prevents many opportunities for an architect's skill set. I understand the significant investment and personal sacrifice required just to have the license to practice, not to mention the additional effort invested in gaining expertise in a specific practice area.

If you don't have the passion for your practice the way it is now, give serious consideration to exploring other options architecture has to offer. Think about the advice you would give to a new architect about choosing a specific area and then give yourself that same advice and follow it. The reality is that the same opportunity exists for every architect, regardless of experience level or years in practice.

This is your life. It's your livelihood. This is where most of your waking hours will be spent, so it'd better be fun, and you'd better want to do it. If there is no passion for the work, then you're setting yourself up to fail because you'll be competing against others who truly believe in what they do. It's not enough to just climb the wall efficiently. Make sure you're climbing the right wall, too.

Once the decision about the practice area has been made, you'll see its significance and implications on many fronts. First, everything else becomes easier. Now, by "easier," we don't mean that everything just magically gets done. What we do mean is that the decision becomes the overriding principle in the business and allows you to say the most important word ever said as you build the practice. That word is "no." Say "no" to all the requests and opportunities that don't further the chosen path. In your role as a business person, many opportunities will come your way. Many will sound amazingly attractive, and more often than not, they promise a life better than what's been chosen, whether it's more money, less work, more prestige, or any other number of appealing scenarios.

But—and this is the hard part—you need to have the conviction in your business decision and the discipline to say "no" to everything that isn't part of the written plan. All those other opportunities, favors, and requests might appear golden on the surface, but in truth, they do nothing but distract the mission, while wasting energy and focus. I've found that those who truly succeed in creating a life they love pick a path and stick to it.

When you say "no," you reinforce your conviction in the chosen path and the decision to pursue your goals. This kind of conviction gives the confidence needed to build the business you want. Saying "no" to rogue opportunities also sends a message to others that you're serious about the plan.

It tells staff, vendors, colleagues, and prospects that there is commitment to the practice and to the mission set forth. The best person to work on your pipes is a plumber, not an electrician. Likewise, the best person to diagnose an illness is a doctor, not a car salesman, and this same concept is true with architects as well. If you want to be a design architect, then that's exactly what you should be. If you want to work designing schools, then that's where you should put all of your efforts. Pick the path and then stick with it. Conviction will resonate throughout your practice.

Your Practice Plan

The next area of planning represents the snapshot of the firm. As Michael puts it, this is the "what we do" piece to the puzzle. This incorporates the revenue goals, the services the practice will provide, the markets it will target, the geographic areas it will reach, and, of course, the realistic time frame needed to accomplish all of these goals. Add to that the location of the office, the initial number of employees, and the anticipated staff growth, and you'll begin to see your practice plan take shape.

Want to really put this planning thing to work? Look forward and project when and how the business will grow. Anticipate what additional services the clients will need or want and, more importantly, be willing to pay for. Actually, this isn't as difficult as it might sound. Learn by asking your existing clients. If the questions are properly framed, the quality of the feedback that your clients will provide will be amazing. After the "what" is figured out, you move on to the details of "how." That is, how can it tactically all happen?

Obviously, there are systems in place for a variety of things, including marketing, converting prospects to clients, and, of course, actually getting the work done. But don't assume that these systems are the same ones from "way back when." In fact, don't even assume that the systems that are in place right now are actually the systems you need to best serve the business.

Doing business in the twenty-first century is a whole new ballgame. The old traditional methods of partner announcements, golf outings, and the old Yellow Page advertisements have given way to an array of new marketing tools. Seminars, direct mail, e-mail, newspaper ads, web sites, and teleconferences are just a sampling of what's available, and that doesn't even touch on the world of social networking.

Marketing in the digital age includes new ways of reaching people, and what's more, these methods are changing and expanding all the time. These new tools allow for interactive communication between the firm and prospects, allowing the public to comment on your services and their experiences with your firm. Some of the most recent popular sites to be considered include LinkedIn, Facebook, Twitter, Blogging, YouTube, etc.

The playing field is constantly changing, so it's difficult to know which platforms will survive. It's impossible to ignore the strength and reach of these new tools. Your architectural firm should consider all of them as the marketing strategy takes shape.

Your Completion Plan

The heart of the business building process will revolve around establishing and documenting systems for every part of the practice. If this sounds like a tedious waste of time, then know this: this step, more than any other, will quickly transform a chaotic and inefficient practice into a real business with a life apart from the owners. I was amazed at the feeling when I felt the power that my systems brought to my business.

So, for every task, every job, and every function that is done in the firm on an even semi-regular basis, there should be a system. There should be a system for developing leads. A system for answering the phone. A system for greeting clients, for setting up the conference room, and for corresponding with clients and engineers. There will be a system for filing documents, as well as a system for hiring new personnel, for giving performance reviews, and for letting a staff member go when their performance isn't meeting the expectations of your practice.

Whatever area you practice in, there should be a well-developed group of systems that details every area of that practice. If an employee leaves and a new one comes on board, they are able to review an operations manual that not only outlines the company's policies and culture, but also documents the proper way to perform their job as well as the way that their performance will be measured. Until those systems are firmly entrenched in the firm, you still just have a practice and not a business.

Now, you might be asking, "What's the point of all this systemization?" Any architect knows how to set up a project, just as any receptionist knows how to greet clients. But that doesn't mean they know your way. You might have some different ideas about how to best get things done, and if you're really interested in transforming the practice into a self-sufficient business, there will certainly be some different ideas.

The completion plan makes sure that everyone is on the same page. It ensures that clients are always greeted in the same manner, even if the receptionist is not available to do the greeting. It guarantees that any project completed by the firm gets done in an efficient and timely manner.

The completion plan allows your practice to evolve by constantly questioning the "way we've always done things" and then looking for the "way we should be doing things" instead. When this type of game plan is implemented, everyone in the firm can get on board. Suddenly, instead of having "people issues," there are system issues, but now you and your staff can tackle those issues together and that creates a major shift in the way you do business.

Staff will feel more confident about the way they do their jobs, and vendors and clients will reap the benefits of your efficiency.

The plan will identify the goal you want to accomplish, outline the steps required to do it, and establish a system for tracking those steps and monitoring performance. In the world of management, there is no easier way to stay on top of the business than this. When these systems are implemented, it's much easier to position your firm as a leader in the marketplace. Trust me on this; I've seen it happen.

Eleven Essential Systems to Dominate Your Market

- Aligning your business with your personal values
- Multiple marketing activities generating an endless supply of qualified prospects
- Inspiring clients to take action and retain your firm
- Designing, presenting, and executing state-of-the-art plans
- Regularly communicating with clients through multiple touches
- Dependable income year after year from every client
- Integration of the best tools to create documents and manage your firm
- Putting the right people with the right skills in the right positions
- Managing by the numbers to keep in touch with your profitability
- Staying on the cutting edge of effective strategies
- Developing multiple sources of revenue

When your firm implements these systems, the transformation from practice to business begins.

With the planning process completed, you can start putting your ideas into action, and that means you need management. So, let's keep going and learn how to manage the plans you've created. ❧

On the Subject of Management

Michael E. Gerber

Good management consists of showing average people how to do the work of superior people.

—John D. Rockefeller

Every architect, including Steve, eventually faces the issues of management. Most face it badly.

Why do so many architects suffer from a kind of paralysis when it comes to dealing with management? Why are so few able to get their architectural company to work the way they want it to and to run it on time? Why are their managers (if they have any) seemingly so inept?

There are two main problems.

First, the architect usually abdicates accountability for management by hiring an office manager. Thus, the architect is working hand-in-glove with someone who is supposed to do the managing. But the architect is unmanageable himself! The architect doesn't think like a manager because he doesn't think he is a manager. He's an architect! He rules the roost. And so he gets the office manager to take care of stuff like scheduling appointments, keeping his calendar, collecting receivables, hiring/firing, and much more.

Second, no matter who does the managing, he or she usually has a completely dysfunctional idea of what it means to manage. They're trying to manage people, contrary to what is needed. We often hear that a good manager must be a "people person." Someone who loves to nourish, figure out, support, care for, teach, baby, monitor, mentor, direct, track, motivate, and, if all else fails, threaten or beat up his or her people.

Don't believe it. Management has far less to do with people than you've been led to believe.

In fact, despite the claims of every management book written by management gurus (who have seldom managed anything), no one—with the exception of a few bloodthirsty tyrants—has ever learned how to manage people.

And the reason is simple: People are almost impossible to manage.

Yes, it's true. People are unmanageable. They're inconsistent, unpredictable, unchangeable, unrepentant, irrepressible, and generally impossible.

Doesn't knowing this make you feel better? Now you understand why you've had all those problems! Do you feel the relief, the heavy stone lifted from your chest?

The time has come to fully understand what management is really all about. Rather than managing people, management is really all about managing a process, a step-by-step way of doing things, which, combined with other processes, becomes a system.

For example:

- The process for on-time scheduling
- The process for answering the telephone
- The process for greeting a client
- The process for organizing client files

Thus, a process is the step-by-step way of doing something over time. Considered as a whole, these processes are a system:

- The on-time scheduling system
- The telephone answering system
- The client greeting system
- The file organization system

Instead of managing people, then, the truly effective manager has been taught a system for managing a process through which people get things done.

More precisely, managers and their people, *together*, manage the processes—the systems—that comprise your business. Management is less about *who* gets things done in your business than about *how* things get done.

In fact, great managers are not fascinated with people but with how things get done through people. Great managers are masters at figuring out how to get things done effectively and efficiently through people using extraordinary systems.

Great managers constantly ask key questions, such as:

- What is the result we intend to produce?
- Are we producing that result every single time?
- If we're not producing that result every single time, why not?
- If we are producing that result every single time, how could we produce even better results?
- Do we lack a system? If so, what would that system look like if we were to create it?
- If we have a system, why aren't we using it?

And so forth.

In short, a great manager can leave the office fully assured that it will run at least as well as it does when he or she is physically in the room. Great managers are those who use a great management system. It is a system that shouts, "This is how we manage here" not "This is who manages here."

In a truly effective company, how you manage is always more important than who manages. Provided a system is in place, how you manage is transferable, whereas who manages isn't. How you manage can be taught, whereas who manages can't be.

When a company is dependent on who manages—Murray, Mary, or Moe—that business is in serious jeopardy. Because when Murray, Mary, or Moe leaves, that business has to start over again. What an enormous waste of time and resources!

Even worse, when a company is dependent on who manages, you can bet all the managers in that business are doing their own thing. What could be more unproductive than ten managers who each manage in a unique way? How in the world could you possible manage those managers?

The answer is: You can't. Because it takes you right back to trying to manage people again.

And, as I hope you now know, that's impossible.

In this chapter, I often refer to managers in the plural. I know that most architects only have one manager—the office manager. And so you may be thinking that a management system isn't so important in a small architectural firm. After all, the office manager does whatever an office manager does (and thank God, because you don't want to do it).

But if your company is ever going to turn into the business it could become, and if that business is ever going to turn into the enterprise of your dreams, then the questions you ask about how the office manager manages your affairs are critical ones. Because until you come to grips with your dual role as owner and key employee, and the relationship your manager has to those two roles, your company/business/enterprise will never realize its potential. Thus the need for a management system.

Management System

What, then, is a management system?

The E-Myth says that a management system is the method by which every manager innovates, quantifies, orchestrates, and then monitors the systems through which your business produces the results you expect.

According to the E-Myth, a manager's job is simple: to invent the systems through which the owner's vision is consistently and faithfully manifested at the operating level of the business.

Which brings us right back to the purpose of your business and the need for an entrepreneurial vision.

Are you beginning to see what I'm trying to share with you? That your business is one single thing? And that all the subjects we're discussing here—money, planning, management, and so on—are all about doing one thing well?

That one thing is the one thing your business is intended to do: distinguish your architectural firm from all others.

It is the manager's role to make certain it all fits. And it's your role as entrepreneur to make sure your manager knows what the business is supposed to look, act, and feel like when it's finally done. As clearly as you know how, you must convey to your manager what you know to be true—your vision, your picture of the business when it's finally done. In this way, your vision is translated into your manager's marching orders every day he or she reports to work.

Unless your manager embraces that vision, you and your people will suffer from the tyranny of routine. And your business will suffer from it too.

Now let's move on to people. Because, as we know, it's people who are causing all our problems. But first let's see how E-Myth management insights affected Norbert's architectural business. ✤

CHAPTER

8

Seemingly Unmanageable

Norbert C. Lemermeyer

It is possible that people need to believe that they are unmanaged if they are managed effectively.

—John Kenneth Galbraith

Most of us in business have read at least one book on the topic. Likely, that book dealt specifically with the subject of management, because there are so many management books to choose from. Shop in your local bookstore and you'll find an overwhelming selection of texts outlining the most current trends in management strategies. These "management strategies" usually translate into motivating employees.

Isn't "management" all about overseeing the people who work for you? You wind up with the problem of playing the roles of a part-time psychiatrist, a babysitter, a priest, and a warden to make management work.

When I began in business, I chose a few of the best I knew to join me in the new firm. Not only were they good technicians, they were also good friends. As colleagues, there was a lot of mutual respect and we got along famously. Once we started to work together, the relationship changed from one of colleagueship to one of owner to employee. I wanted things done in a certain way and since they were colleagues, they felt that they had equal input into how the business was run and how architecture would be practiced in my office.

To begin with, there were no systems in place, so all the authority came directly from me. There were only very basic office policies and guidelines about how the work was to be done. Before long there was a power struggle, and not long after that, the respect evaporated and the friendship came to an end. Needless to say, before long, they, along with their expertise, left the firm.

That's when I bought my first book on management.

My next set of employees were young graduates of technical schools and schools of architecture. It was my thought, since they were inexperienced, that I could mold them to my way of thinking. It took years to develop a team who worked in the way I wanted to practice architecture. In spite of their developing skills and experience, I still had day-to-day supervision. I had to work long hours teaching, supervising, and laying out the projects in terms of schedules and work assignments. During the day, I spent time on business development and other aspects of running a business, so the only time I had to lay out the projects so staff could work on them was evenings and weekends. This created stress in my personal life and resentment in the office, as the employees spent time with their loved ones and their hobbies while I spent my nights and weekends keeping the business going effectively.

After a few years I developed a team I had trained who were permitting me some free time. One Monday morning, just when I thought things were starting to go well again, my best technician came into my office and said he was moving to another firm in town. After all the training I had given him, he was moving on to one of my competitors, who would benefit from my efforts. It took nearly five years to train this man and now I was faced with starting all over again. It wasn't long before the remainder of the team also decided to move on. I was devastated.

That's when I bought my second book on management.

Anyway, I hired a new staff of new graduates and experienced technicians. I began to practice what I had learned in my management studies: providing a friendly working environment, flexible hours, input into how the work was done, etc. This worked to an extent; however, getting this method going and keeping it going took many hours—nights and weekends. If I managed to take a holiday, it would be for only a week—not enough time to de-stress. After another five-year period, I again had built a strong team who were executing satisfactorily. That's when the economy hit a recession and I had to lay off my staff, who I had trained personally to fit the way I practiced architecture.

Over and over this cycle repeated itself. I felt it was my inability to manage my staff and provide an environment in which they would feel they belonged, one that they would be proud of and work hard to maintain. I was spending too much time on staff management, so the other aspects of running the business were faltering, especially business development. This led to increased stress. In spite of the time I spent, my success with management of staff wasn't getting anywhere. I felt I was doomed to failure, as I couldn't keep all aspects of the business going successfully.

By this time I'd spent nearly twenty years in business. During this time, to no avail, I'd read over twenty books on business management. I decided to take some time off and review my management style and ask myself some serious questions.

What if I've been focused on the wrong problem? What if the staff wasn't the issue? What if it was my systems or lack of systems instead? What if I was usurping control rather than dispensing it? The answers to these questions put a whole new spin on things.

Now, instead of trying to manage a group of distinctly unique individuals, all of whom have their own set of ideas, motivators and emotions, I now manage a set of systems, which are analytical, not emotional. Systems don't require motivation or nurturing to work, and are designed by me.

This breakthrough way of thinking was first presented by Michael E. Gerber in his book, *The E-Myth*. He discovered it while observing the extraordinary success of fast food pioneer McDonald's. Somehow, they needed to turn pimply-faced, ADD, teenaged kids into productive workers in charge of multimillion-dollar franchises, and you know what? They did it!

As Michael describes it, "They come in late, leave early and smoke dope during lunch." They have a thousand-percent turnover of employees, and still these same workers produce record profits and make owning a McDonald's franchise the closest thing to owning a money-making machine.

So, how did they accomplish such an impossible feat? Certainly not by trying to control hormone-ravaged teenagers, but rather by focusing on the systems for doing things with a step-by-step written blueprint for every task. The steps for making French fries, greeting customers, cleaning up, and tracking cash are documented in detail for every staff member to see. In short, a written manual that most likely includes multi-media learning tools provides documentation and training for every new hire who walks through the door. If one worker leaves, a new one can be up and running, producing identical results, whether they're in Buffalo or Bangkok. Now that's a system!

As I said, I re-read *The E-Myth*. I enrolled in E-Myth Mastery, an online program set up by Michael E. Gerber. In this program, you complete a lesson having to do with one aspect of business, send it to an online business coach, and discuss it in a telephone meeting. Faithfully I completed the lessons over a two-year time period. Not only did I complete the lessons, but I incorporated each lesson into my business operations.

This meant, for the most part, writing systems for each aspect of the business. As each system was written, it was incorporated into the business practice by training staff to follow written systems. It took effort to change the culture of word-of-mouth, daily work assignments to a systems-based set of processes for all staff members to follow. Not only were they working following a set of systems, they were systematically being evaluated according to their use of the systems.

It didn't take long, once the early systems were being used, that their effect could be felt. Production of our work was smoother, there were fewer mistakes, less conflict, and, most importantly, more work got done with less and less of my input as the systems came on stream. This meant I had more free time to either work on the business or just take weekends off. It took nearly three years for all the systems to be written, tested, rolled out, and put into practice in my office.

Last year, I had nearly three months off, traveling the world without any worries whether the work was being done or the clients were being looked after. This would have been unheard of before we had revolutionized the firm using the principles outlined in *The E-Myth*. The systems effectively give the guidance for all team members to follow to complete their work with minimum input. The way the business runs now, I am enjoying the practice of architecture, my staff is happy and committed, clients are better served, there is more time to work on the business; thus it is more successful in every way. My pre-E-Myth days of stress, sarcasm, despondency, aggravation, and hopelessness have turned into excitement and optimism—feelings I haven't had since I left the school of architecture.

It doesn't matter whether you're a doctor, a banker, an architect, or a retail firm, any business will benefit when they choose to manage systems rather than people. The transformation of my business through the E-Myth is an example of how a business can become a source of pride and achievement for its owner. Based on my experience and talking to other people, the following are some observations.

High quality personnel in your firm are valuable, most certainly. But the majority of your focus should still be in creating innovative systems that you can measure and monitor. Once those systems are in place, it becomes much easier to find world-class employees who can make them work. What's more, employees who might otherwise have been passed over often blossom into productive staff members when given a turnkey system like the one we're describing here. I've seen it happen over and over again. This makes hiring new employees a much easier prospect.

Like most architects, I would obsess with finding experienced workers, including receptionists, technologists, spec writers, and even other architects in the firm. I now take a different view. I find people with the right personalities and character traits for each type of job—people who possess key attributes that can't be taught, like friendliness, perseverance, and great interpersonal skills, balanced with eagerness to learn and a desire to take on responsibility—and then marry those people to my set of innovative systems and watch the firm begin to transform!

Obviously, you'll want to have workers who possess basic skills in their field, but in all honesty, most of those skills can be taught. I find that it's easier to teach a bright, inexperienced, technologist the skills they'll need in your architectural firm, than to try undo the bad habits that a more experienced person might bring from some other dysfunctional firm. Many of these employees resist change, which means they're also resisting growth. I tell them thanks, but no thanks, and tell them to move on. My firm and my innovative staff will thank me for it.

When I ask architects to describe the positions in their firm and their employees who currently hold the jobs, the conversation invariably goes the same way. They'll describe the personalities, work habits, and general opinions about each employee.

I've never once heard an architect talk about the systems in place that represent how they do things in their firm. They might lament Jane's shortcomings or sing Tom's praises, but that's where the analysis stops. Interestingly, they don't realize that even if they had a firm filled with Toms, they would be no closer to having a well-managed business.

The reason they don't realize this is because Tom is doing his job, and it's a great job at that. But someday, Tom will leave the firm, just like every other great employee working for you at this very moment. Whether it's because of illness, a move, a better job, pregnancy, or some other reason, it's rare that an employee spends his or her entire career with the same firm.

When the great employee does decide to leave, the architect suddenly realizes that all that wisdom and experience they held so dear has just walked out the door. What to do, what to do? As I said, this was a repeating pattern in my office.

Tom knew where all the project files were kept. He knew how to set up a project, deal with the consultants, and solve all sorts of site problems. Now Tom's gone, and since even the best employee typically gives a whole two weeks' notice, you don't have much time to replace your star employee.

Can you possibly recruit, hire, and train that replacement in two weeks? Probably not. Which means that your best worker crippled your architectural firm. Not intentionally, of course, but that's the way it worked out. Had your systems been in place, however, training a replacement would be a snap. Tom's leaving wouldn't equate to years of knowledge lost. The firm's wisdom is not in the employees but in the systems. Your firm will not only survive Tom leaving, but it will continue to prosper as well.

I've seen it happen over and over, and I'll tell you what I tell other architects: without systems, your best workers are potentially your biggest obstacle to having a great business.

Crafting a New Vision

With the right systems, your architectural firm will be re-created to reflect your vision about your practice of architecture. Are you going to make your firm unique? Why should prospective clients pick your firm over all the others? What special place will your practice occupy in the community?

In the beginning, maybe it was just about the money. Get the clients in the door and start generating as many fees as you can.

But we all know that's not a sustainable business model, and more importantly, will not ultimately serve you or your clients.

When you implement systems, you create a machine that works independently of you. You give your employees the roadmap they need to do things that need to get done.

- This is how we greet clients.
- This is how we prepare construction documents.
- This is how we prepare the construction phase of the work.
- This is how we manage a start-up meeting.
- This is how we handle finances.
- This is how we handle billings.
- This is how we generate leads and convert them into clients.
- This is how we hire people.

And so on and so on.

If you go back and look at the planning process we discussed earlier, you'll quickly see that the "what" is far more important than the "who." But before you can have a business that truly serves your needs, you need to know what that business is. You need to define the "what" piece of your firm's puzzle. Now that we've established the importance of managing your systems, let's see how that plays out with the people in your firm.❧

CHAPTER

9

On the Subject
of People

Michael E. Gerber

Very few people go to the doctor when they have a cold. They go to the theatre instead.

—Oscar Wilde

Every architect I've ever met has complained about people.

About employees: "They come in late, they use the company trucks to go visit their girlfriends, they smoke dope at lunch time, steal gasoline and they go home early. They have the focus of an antique camera!"

About subcontractors: "Who knows what they do with their time—but they certainly know how to charge for it!"

About suppliers: "They can never make deliveries on time!"

About their clients: "They want me to repair years of bad habits and inadequate building maintenance!" or "Even if they had a mind, they wouldn't be able to make it up!"

People, people, people. Every architect's nemesis. And at the heart of it all are the people who work for you.

"By the time I tell them how to do it, I could have done it twenty times myself!" "How come nobody listens to what I say?" "Why is it nobody ever does what I ask them to do?"

Does this sound like you?

So what's the problem with people? To answer that, think back to the last time you walked into a architect's office. What did you see in the people's faces?

Most people working in architecture are harried. You can see it in their expressions. They're negative. They're tired. They're humorless. And with good reason! After all, they're surrounded by people all day long who have money problems, marital issues, or trouble with their children.

Clients are looking for nurturing, for empathy, for care. And many are frustrated with not getting the same level of respect from their clients.

Is it any wonder employees at most architectural firms are disgruntled? They're surrounded by unhappy people all day. They're answering the same questions 24/7. And most of the time, the owner or the manager has no time for them. He or she is too busy leading a dysfunctional life.

Working with people brings great joy—and monumental frustration. And so it is with architects and their people. But why? And what can we do about it?

Let's look at the typical architect—who this person is and isn't.

Most architects are unprepared to use other people to get results. Not because they can't find people, but because they are fixated on getting the results themselves. In other words, most architects are not the businesspeople they need to be, but technicians suffering from an entrepreneurial seizure.

Am I talking about you? What were you doing before you became an entrepreneur?

Were you an architect working at a large, multi-office organization? A midsized company? A small practice?

Didn't you imagine owning your own company as the way out?

Didn't you think that because you knew how to do the technical work—because you knew so much about building design, planning, and drawing images to scale—that you were automatically prepared to create a company that does that type of work?

Didn't you figure that by creating your own sole proprietorship you could dump the boss once and for all? How else to get rid of that impossible person, the one driving you crazy, the one who never let you do your own thing, the one who was the main reason you decided to take the leap into a business of your own in the first place?

Didn't you start your own company so you could become your own boss?

And didn't you imagine that once you became your own boss, you would be free to do whatever you wanted to do—and to take home all the money?

Honestly, isn't that what you imagined? So you went into business for yourself and immediately dived into work.

Doing it, doing it, doing it.

Busy, busy, busy.

Until one day you realized (or maybe not) that you were doing all of the work. You were doing everything you knew how to do, plus a lot more you knew nothing about. Building sweat equity, you thought.

In reality, you were a technician suffering from an entrepreneurial seizure.

You were just hoping to make a buck in your own company. And sometimes you did earn a wage. But other times you didn't. You were the one signing the checks, all right, but they went to other people.

Does this sound familiar? Is it driving you crazy?

Well, relax, because we're going to show you the right way to do it this time.

Read carefully. Be mindful of the moment. You are about to learn the secret you've been waiting for all your working life.

The People Law

It's critical to know this about the working life of architects who own their own architectural firm: Without people, you don't own a company, you own a job. And it can be the worst job in the world because you're working for a lunatic! (Nothing personal—but we've got to face facts.)

Let me say what every architect knows: Without people, you're going to have to do it all yourself. Without human help, you're doomed to try to do too much. This isn't a breakthrough idea, but it's amazing how many architects ignore the truth. They end up knocking themselves out, ten to twelve hours a day. They try to do more, but less actually gets done.

The load can double you over and leave you panting. In addition to the work you're used to doing, you may also have to do the books. And the organizing. And the filing. You'll have to do the planning and the scheduling. When you own your own company, the daily minutiae are never ceasing—as I'm sure you've found out. Like painting the Golden Gate Bridge, it's endless. Which puts it beyond the realm of human possibility. Until you discover how to get it done by somebody else, it will continue on and on until you're a burned-out husk.

But with others helping you, things will start to drastically improve. If, that is, you truly understand how to engage people in the work you need them to do. When you learn how to do that, when you learn how to replace yourself with other people—people trained in your system—then your company can really begin to grow. Only then will you begin to experience true freedom yourself.

What typically happens is that architects, knowing they need help answering the phone, filing, and so on, go out and find people who can do these things. Once they delegate these duties, however, they rarely spend any time with the hoi polloi. Deep down, they feel it's not important how these things get done; it's only important that they get done.

They fail to grasp the requirement for a system that makes people their greatest asset rather than their greatest liability. A system so reliable that if Chris dropped dead tomorrow, Leslie could do exactly what Chris did. That's where the People Law comes in.

The People Law says that each time you add a new person to your company using an intelligent (turnkey) system that works, you expand your reach. And you can expand your reach almost infinitely! People allow you to be everywhere you want to be simultaneously, without actually having to be there in the flesh.

People are to an architect what a record was to Frank Sinatra. A Sinatra record could be (and still is) played in a million places at the same time, regardless of where he was. And every record sale produced royalties for Sinatra (or his estate). With the help of other people, Sinatra created a quality recording that faithfully replicated his unique talents, then made sure it was marketed and distributed, and the revenue managed.

Your people can do the same thing for you. All you need to do is to create a "recording"—a system—of your unique talents, your special way of practicing architecture, and then replicate it, market it, distribute it, and manage the revenue.

Isn't that what successful businesspeople do? Make a "recording" of their most effective ways of doing business? In this way, they provide a turnkey solution to their clients' problems. A system solution that really works.

Doesn't your company offer the same potential for you that records did for Sinatra (and now for his heirs): The ability to produce income without having to go to work every day?

Isn't that what your people could be for you? The means by which your system for practicing architecture could be faithfully replicated?

But first you've got to have a system. You have to create a unique way of doing business that you can teach to your people, that you can manage faithfully, and that you can replicate consistently, just like McDonald's.

Because without such a system, without such a "recording," without a unique way of doing business that really works, all you're left with is people doing their own thing. And that is almost always a recipe for chaos. Rather than guaranteeing consistency, it encourages mistake after mistake after mistake.

And isn't that how the problem started in the first place? People doing whatever they perceived they needed to do, regardless of what you wanted? People left to their own devices with no regard for the costs of their behavior? The costs to you?

In other words, people without a system.

Can you imagine what would have happened to Frank Sinatra if he had followed that example? If every one of his recordings had been done differently? Imagine a million different versions of "My Way." It's unthinkable.

Would you buy a record like that? What if Frank was having a bad day? What if he had a sore throat?

Please hear this: The People Law is unforgiving. Without a systematic way of doing business, people are more often a liability than an asset. Unless you prepare, you'll find out too late which ones are which.

The People Law says that without a specific system for doing business; without a specific system for recruiting, hiring, and training your people to use that system; and without a specific system for managing and improving your systems, your company will always be a crapshoot.

Do you want to roll the dice with your company at stake? Unfortunately, that is what most architects are doing.

The People Law also says that you can't effectively delegate your responsibilities unless you have something specific to delegate. And that something specific is a way of doing business that works!

Frank Sinatra is gone, but his voice lives on. And someone is still counting his royalties. That's because Sinatra had a system that worked.

Do you? Now move on to the subject architects. But first let's see what Norbert has to say about people. ✤

People Make
It Happen

Norbert C. Lemermeyer

People can be divided into three groups: those who make things happen,
those who watch things happen, and those who wonder what happened.
— John Newbern

With your systems now in place, you can now turn your attention to the essence of your business, also known as your people.

Properly trained technologists are able to do a big percentage of what must be done in an architectural firm. Too many architects are doing things that are better left to staff, and the result is that the firm doesn't run as smoothly as it could, regardless of how well the workload is managed.

As Michael says, "Without people, you don't own a practice—you own a job."

Certainly, for some architects, having a high-paying job is exactly what they want, and they do this by working in someone else's firm where they can focus on the doing it, doing it, doing it, while other people handle everything else. They spend their days designing, putting together presentations, attending conferences, and honing their architectural skills. And there's nothing wrong with that.

If you aspire to own your own business in architecture, or perhaps want to revamp the one you have, you gave up that employee mentality a long time ago. You want to control your own destiny, come and go as you please, say yes to some clients and show others the door. You desire a entrepreneurial life with all its potential payoffs and riches.

But, you've probably found out, going from employee to businessman isn't that easy. As an architect-businessman you work long hours on nights and weekends, sometimes with very little to show for your efforts. Your stress level is high—exponentially higher than in your life as an employee—and it's created havoc in your personal life.

This is where people can help. Not just any people, but your people you have successfully integrated into your systems processes.

How I Began In Business

When I first began my practice, there was no doubt that I needed people to help complete the work—technicians, a receptionist, a bookkeeper, and architects. In my mind I had a clear idea of how the practice should work, providing architectural services. In the beginning, the power of being a leader and business owner was very gratifying.

I wanted my stamp on all the work when it was competed. The workflow, the design, the finances. The policies and the procedures all had to be done my way. Many meetings were held individually or in groups where I would verbally outline how the work was to be done. If the work was not executed my way, I repeated instructions. For various reasons, my instructions were not heard and not followed, as they had their own opinions of how to do the work. As there was nothing in writing, the instructions were easily misinterpreted or forgotten or argued.

As years went by, I spent more time on projects and office affairs, keeping a tight rein on every project and on every aspect of the office operations. Sometimes it felt like I was running a kindergarten where instructions needed to be repeated daily and minute-by-minute supervision was required. The power and gratification of having a staff became a nightmare.

I became bitter and non-trusting of employees. The employees became frustrated and dissatisfied in their work as they weren't permitted to work independently and achieve fulfillment in their work. Staff turnover was very high. Many newcomers, because of their experience in my office, left the profession. Others left to join another firm in hopes of finding a more suitable working environment. I was in a constant cycle of recruiting, hiring, and training.

For over fifteen years this cycle kept repeating itself. It finally dawned on me that, just possibly, I was the problem. I often visited business establishments where there appeared to be harmony between the employees and employer, high productivity, and upbeat morale. I enviously read annual business reports about fifty great companies to work for. This is what I wanted in my firm.

What I Did

There had to be a way to achieve the state where employees were satisfied, productive, and loyal and employers felt they had a team that could effectively execute the work. I started by reading a number to how-to management books on this subject. They were often quite theoretical and none of them had a clear means to this end. In 1995, *The E-Myth* was recommended to me by a business coach, who I'd hired to help me. He guaranteed, if I structured my business as outlined in *The E-Myth*, I would experience a marked improvement in how the business ran. I altered a number of my business practices. The following list is a list of items that pertained to the human resources—my people:

- I drew up an organization chart showing the business hierarchy clearly, along with titled positions.

- For each position, there was a written list of responsibilities and accountabilities.

- A simple set of systems was written describing how the work was to be executed.

- Specific tasks would be outlined in writing along with an agreed-to completion date in what came to be known as the Delegation System.

Within six months after setting these simple systems in place, there was a marked improvement within the staff. For the first time in my office we began to feel like a team where each person knew his/her role and the specific roles of others. Projects were satisfactorily completed with less of my involvement in less time. Less of my involvement meant I was working fewer hours, fewer evenings, and fewer weekends.

At first, my staff, my people, and the engine that drove my office were skeptical of the new ways according to the E-Myth. When they caught on, they became advocates. These rudimentary systems, which at first seemed slow and awkward, were their tickets to independence and fulfillment in the office. They felt more in charge of the work in the office and I felt the work was being done my way. A win-win.

As these basic systems took hold, the office became very productive and busy. Rather than continuing to refine and develop systems, I reverted to doing the work again. There was slippage in the systems, and by 2004 there was very little left and we were back to the old cycle of hiring, training, and losing good staff.

In 2005, I was near retirement age, but I felt that, even though I was marginally successful, I had something left to prove in this life by establishing a successful office. This I defined as the following:

- A continuous, sustainable flow of work

- A business where I needed to only work normal hours and was able to take long holidays, yet for the office to function in accordance with my priorities

- A business where I could control the way work was completed

- A satisfied and loyal staff who enjoyed working for me

In 2006, I signed up with the E-Myth Mastery program. I was asked in 2007 to join a new upstart firm. I agreed on the condition that we follow the exact outline as written in the Mastery program. This program outlines a business completely set up and run by systems from top to bottom. Based on our earlier attempts at system development, we set up a program to completely systematize our operations. Most of the systems are now in place, but we find that in the normal course of business, additional systems are required. Our systems are monitored regularly and revised as required. We are now at the end of year four of a planned five-year start-up program.

What Happened

From the staff aspect of the business, we've succeeded to where we now have satisfied staff who are young, eager, loyal, and know they are getting ahead. They are proud of the company's achievements and act as if the business is their own. We have a strong set of systems designed to ensure that our staff will continue to be strong long into the future. Because of what's in place—the people systems—we can now build a company knowing we will have a strong staff component to complete the work when we need them. The systems ensuring these things are as follows:

- A complete organizational chart outlining the company
- Detailed position descriptions of responsibilities and accountabilities
- Recruitment process
- Hiring process
- Orientation process
- Education and development systems
- Evaluation and feedback systems
- Annual staff performance review

This set of systems, combined with other company systems, guarantee that our firm, along with its people, will get stronger each year, long into the future. Now that these systems are in place, one of my most enjoyable tasks in the office is teaching and training. With this training, which is part of the education system, new employees quickly become independent and are trusted to take on tasks within the context of the office. After orientation, the production systems guide newcomers to effectiveness and independence much quicker than without orientation.

What a change from years ago, when I supervised each employee's every move. You can see how the hours I spend at the office are much shorter and my holidays much longer. Best of all, the hours I do spend at the office are much more enjoyable, being surrounded by motivated employees who know exactly

The application process is designed to help you organize prospective employee information. Yes, you must always get the basics of contact information and educational and work history. But that's not enough. For you to identify superstars, you need to put the standard application on steroids. You need to challenge the candidate with practical tests. The application tests should include horticultural questions, tool identification, math problems, situational responses, and writing answers to open-ended questions. These tests, which should focus on the technical portion of your company's work, begin the screening process.

The Faces of Your Firm

A primary reason that architects want to perform many tasks in the office is that they want them consistently completed in a certain way. In the past the only way to ensure this was direct supervision each and every step of the way. If I must do this to ensure getting things done my way, the architect says, I might as well do it myself. So he does.

You can imagine how curious architects are to learn how much of their work can be delegated. What could possibly free up that much time? We want to know what it is. Almost all construction-related tasks can be handled by a well-trained technologist with a winning personality.

What makes this change work is having a system in place to handle this task. There is no reason why the architect must be present for or attend to the construction-related tasks; they've just assumed that they are needed for these tasks because they know what needs to be done.

But once the system is established, a good technologist can handle the process without blinking an eye. For any architect who's screaming, "That won't work," yes, there are some exceptions to the rule. But you're missing this point: delegating tasks that don't require your personal attention can free up your calendar.

That means more time for the architect to work on all those architect-only issues. Just by making that one change, these architects have expanded their ability to do business efficiently. And should that technologist one day decide to leave, you have a system in place that allows your new technologist to pick up right where the other left off.

This is the real secret behind business success. Not only does your business run more efficiently, but your staff becomes happier as well. Who doesn't want happy staff? Remember, your technologist chose that career path because he or she wanted to do technologist kinds of things, not just to sit around and take orders for every task. All architects want to practice architecture and not fill their days with technical or clerical duties.

Most architects will agree that a properly trained technologist who loves being with people is better at the job than are the architects themselves. Clients then get to bond with the firm, not just you, so when they have routine questions, they'll be comfortable talking to your technologist instead of insisting on speaking to you personally. Can you see just how much time you could save by making this one change?

Once you've implemented your systems, you can address the issue of who will do what. This is where management can really be fun. Filling the positions in your firm is similar to working a jigsaw puzzle. You want the right piece in the right place for the puzzle to come together as a whole.

Ironically, the front desk position is often an afterthought for architects, when in truth, it's that position that essentially holds the key to your firm's first impression. Many architects make a big mistake by putting the least-qualified people in that spot and then paying them poorly to boot. Yet the front desk is often the first contact that prospects and clients have with your firm, so you definitely want someone who is suited to welcome people into your office.

This is true with any position in your firm. As you start fitting people with your various systems, make sure you look beyond skills and match personalities and talents to the job as well. When you do this, you create a staff that has a vested interest in your firm's success. They know that their job is an integral part of your architectural practice, even if they aren't actually practicing architecture.

This knowledge instills things like pride and loyalty—qualities that most certainly can transform an office full of people into an efficient and innovative staff. Now, which one would you like to work with?

This process of bringing people on board is essentially your hiring system. It will outline how you solicit candidates, how they are interviewed, and what tests should be administered, as well as how you'll check references and do background investigations.

One incredibly valuable part of a good hiring system is something called a "group interview." For most positions in the firm this method will save lots of time for both you and the candidates. This system is resisted by architects until they see how quickly it zeroes in on the people that they really want to interview one-on-one.

Here's how it works: When you have a position to be filled in your firm, a series of events must take place. An ad appears, whether it's in the newspaper or on the web, and interested candidates send in their resumes. You review the qualifications and schedule individual interviews. This can be incredibly time-consuming, and if your experiences are like ours, some people don't show up, and in the cases of others, you wish they hadn't bothered. We rarely terminate the interview within the first few minutes, even when we know it's a waste of time because we feel obligated to "hear them out."

In a group interview, you invite all of the candidates who pass the first round of resume reviews at the same time. You set up a room at your firm (your delightful receptionist could handle that task for you!), and a trusted staff member makes a presentation about your firm, its culture, and the nature of the position you're offering. Once the introduction is done, you can now ask the group if there is anyone who is not interested in the job. For those who remain, and in our experience it will be most of them, you can start asking open-ended questions to the applicants.

Here's where the magic begins. Something remarkable happens in the "back and forth" that goes on between the people in the room. You get an opportunity to see how they interact with each other and with your team. You get to see whether they are outgoing, articulate, reserved, how they dress, how they carry themselves, and a hundred other little characteristics that you might not have seen in a one-on-one. Once the meeting is over, you can huddle with your team and decide which of the group are worthy of a further interview. Those who would never have made the cut are skimmed off early. Again, this is one of those best practices that architects initially resist but totally embrace once they give it a try. It's also another example of why it's important to rethink the way you do business.

Now, all this glowing hype aside, you must still have a system for personality and skill testing of the candidates, even with the group interview method. This is because most people hire for all the wrong reasons. Some like the candidate and go with their gut, while others tend to hire employees who are just like them. Most often, people are under a time crunch and simply don't bother with the investigation part of the process.

Typically, this happens because there is not a system in place for hiring. What's more, often there are no systems in place at all. As a result, there is a huge panic when someone leaves. The firm feels the need to fill the position quickly, which usually amounts to getting a warm body in that chair.

But as we've already seen, this is a recipe for disaster, a recipe you won't be following anymore, will you? Now, just because you've found the person you want to hire, doesn't mean the hiring process is over. Quite the contrary, there's still much to do with a new employee. See why a few good systems can come in handy?

A new employee needs to be introduced to your firm's benefit package if you have one. Someone needs to ensure that he fills out all the appropriate forms and that accounting is notified of his employment so he can get paid. You then need another system to ensure that what you hired is truly what you wanted. This is where monitoring those systems can help you out.

No matter how much you test or how much you interview, you can never be certain you've made the right decision until they're actually on the job! After over fifty years of combined hiring experience in hiring employees, we know that the best thing you can do is increase the odds of a proper hire by going through all the steps we've just outlined above. But even then, there are no guarantees.

To counter this uncertainty, you're going to use some of those glorious systems to help you monitor your new employee's progress and ensure that they're truly a good fit for your firm. To do this, you'll need to create a set of questions that the new hire answers each day for the first twenty days of employment. You can decide what the questions are for your firm, but here are a few that have worked before:

- Did you understand what was expected of you today?
- Were you able to accomplish your work today?
- What challenges did you face?
- What resources do you need to help you do your job better?

During those first twenty days, have the new employee send you a report answering those questions. In addition to providing the answers you need, this daily procedure will show you whether the person can follow instructions and whether she is comfortable with reporting her activities.

A major problem I've seen in architectural firms is the architect and/or management does not take the time to follow up with their new hires. These employees are simply shown to their desk and given their list of responsibilities. The rest is up to them.

But this is the time when coaching and feedback are the most effective. Your new employee hasn't developed any systems of his own yet, so now is the time to stay close and guide him along. This is also the time that you can determine if you made the right choice. Granted, all new people will have a learning curve, but if you're not seeing the performance you expected, well, what you see is generally what you get.

That then leaves you with two choices: keep the mediocre employee around to avoid having to hire someone new or cut that person loose and move on. Obviously, it's your call, but if you want the right people, you have to be willing to let a few of the wrong ones go. ❧

11

On the Subject of Associates

Michael E. Gerber

All animals are equal, but some animals are more equal than others.

—George Orwell

I f you're a sole practitioner—that is, you're selling only yourself—then your architectural firm called a "practice" will never make the leap to an architectural firm called a "business." The progression from practice to business to enterprise demands that you hire other architects to do what you do (or don't do). Contractors call these people subcontractors; for our purposes, we'll refer to them as associate architects.

Contractors know that subs can be a huge problem. It's no less true for architects. Until you face this special business problem, your practice will never become a business, and your business will certainly never become an enterprise.

Long ago, God said, "Let there be architects. And so they never forget who they are in my creation, let them be damned forever to hire people exactly like themselves." Enter the associates.

Merriam-Webster's Collegiate Dictionary, Eleventh Edition, defines *sub* as "under, below, secretly; inferior to." If associate architects are like sub-architects, you could define an associate as "an inferior individual contracted to perform part or all of another's contract."

In other words, you, the architect, make a conscious decision to hire someone "inferior" to you to fulfill *your* commitment to *your* client, for which you are ultimately and solely liable.

Why in the world do we do these things to ourselves? Where will this madness lead? It seems the blind are leading the blind, and the blind are paying others to do it. And when an architect is blind, you *know* there's a problem.

It's time to step out of the darkness and come into the light. Forget about being Mr. Nice Guy—it's time to do things that work.

Solving the Associate Architect Problem

Let's say you're about to hire an associate architect. Someone who has specific skills: drafting, designing, whatever. It all starts with choosing the right personnel. After all, these are people to whom you are delegating your responsibility and for whose behavior you are completely liable. Do you really want to leave that choice to chance? Are you that much of a gambler? I doubt it.

If you've never worked with your new associate, how do you really know he or she is skilled? For that matter, what does "skilled" mean?

For you to make an intelligent decision about this associate architect, you must have a working definition of the word *skilled.* Your challenge is to know *exactly* what your expectations are, then to make sure your other architects operate with precisely the same expectations. Failure here almost assures a breakdown in your relationship.

I want you to write the following on a piece of paper: "By *skilled,* I mean ..." Once you create your personal definition, it will become a standard for you and your practice, for your clients, and for your associate architects.

A standard, according to *Webster's Eleventh*, is something "set up and established by authority as a rule for the measure of quantity, weight, extent, value, or quality."

Thus, your goal is to establish a measure of quality control, a standard of skill, which you will apply to all your associate architects. More important, you are also setting a standard for the performance of your company.

By creating standards for your selection of other architects—standards of skill, performance, integrity, financial stability, and experience—you have begun the powerful process of building a practice that can operate exactly as you expect it to.

By carefully thinking about exactly what to expect, you have already begun to improve your practice.

In this enlightened state, you will see the selection of your associates as an opportunity to define what you (1) intend to provide for your clients, (2) expect from your employees, and (3) demand for your life.

Powerful stuff, isn't it? Are you up to it? Are you ready to feel your rising power?

Don't rest on your laurels just yet. Defining those standards is only the first step you need to take. The second step is to create an *associate architect development system.*

An associate architect development system is an action plan designed to tell you what you are looking for in an associate. It includes the exact benchmarks, accountabilities, timing of fulfillment, and budget you will assign to the process of looking for associate architects, identifying them, recruiting them, interviewing them, training them, managing their work, auditing their performance, compensating them, reviewing them regularly, and terminating or rewarding them for their performance.

All of these things must be documented—actually *written down*—if they're going to make any difference to you, your associate architects, your managers, or your bank account!

And then you've got to persist with that system, come hell or high water. Just as Ray Kroc did. Just as Walt Disney did. Just as Sam Walton did.

This leads us to our next topic of discussion: the subject of *estimating*. But first, let's listen to what Norbert has to say on the subject of associate architects. ✤

An Architect's View

Norbert C. Lemermeyer

The best executive is one who has sense enough to pick good men to do what he wants done, and self-restraint enough to keep from meddling with them while they do it.

—Theodore Roosevelt

Depending upon the current situation, the vision, and the future goals of your business will determine whether your business needs to hire an associate architect. Also, your personal goals, outlook, and future plans have a bearing on this decision. An associate architect can have the greatest impact upon a business—either positive or negative—of any position in your firm. Choose wisely for the right reasons.

My Experience

In the early years of my business as an architect, I had numerous associate architects. Some were newly graduated students and wanted to complete their required apprenticeship. Some were fully registered architects. Most often they were hired as designers, as I needed this expertise most as I personally was too occupied with all other aspects of the business. As they were architects, they had their own ideas of how the practice should run. And since there were no written systems or policies in place to guide them, they took their own directions. This resulted in conflict; this is my office, we're going to do things my way. Not to mention, they were doing design work, something that I wanted to do, while I did the not-so-glorious day-to-day work of running the office.

If I made comments on their work, it became a power struggle of equals. Needless to say, none of these relationships worked out to mutual satisfaction.

Before reorganization, most of the work in the office was completed by technicians under my direction. Because my time was limited, our work gravitated to the technical side of architecture. This was not to my complete satisfaction; however, we managed to keep the business going, sometimes quite profitably. Through the years I longed for an associate that could assist me and still practice the way I intended. The associate architect would help by providing design expertise and strength. With the right associate I could take the time to pursue other interests, which the day-to-day running of the office didn't permit. Also, I longed to take more time off than a week here and a week there, to enjoy life, traveling the world.

This associate would have to be a qualified architect who would subscribe to my way of running the business. How could this be accomplished? Next is a discussion around hiring an associate for your firm, followed by a list of items to consider when hiring an associate.

Hiring An Associate

How do you know whom to hire? And how do you know if an associate is really what your firm needs? Your firm will need an associate when it's ready to support an associate and the need for one is clarified. What does that mean?

There's actually a couple of different ways to define "support," so let's start with the easiest one. Clearly, your firm will need to have enough work to keep a new associate busy; that's a given. Your firm will also need to generate enough income to pay your new associate without causing the firm any financial strain, another relatively obvious requirement.

Do you really need more architects in your firm or just a little more efficient way of doing things? Now, we're not suggesting that adding an architect to your staff isn't a good idea. It might be just what your firm needs to continue on its evolutionary path. But before you can make that decision, you should feel confident that you are using your non-architect staff to their full potential.

It makes no sense to hire an associate if you've got qualified non-architect staff that could do the job instead, which raises the question of how you see an associate fitting into your firm's big picture. What will her/his role be? How will she complement what you already do?

Obviously, if you're hiring an associate to handle tasks that could be assumed by your technologist, you're not choosing the most efficient path. You're also almost certainly guaranteeing that your associate (and quite likely your technologist) will eventually get frustrated and leave for greener, and perhaps more satisfying, pastures.

But let's assume that you do in fact have enough architect-only work to warrant hiring an associate. Let's also assume that you run a lean, mean machine and every member of your staff enjoys a rewarding, challenging position in your firm. Does that mean it's time to hire an associate? Can your firm provide the support that a new associate needs to succeed?

Working within the concept of building a business rather than a practice, a new associate will need feedback and guidance as he/she acclimates to your way of doing business.

Is your firm in a position to provide these things? If you don't yet have your basic systems in place (like the ones we've already discussed), then your new associate will be nothing more than another random employee doing his or her own thing. Kind of defeats the purpose of hiring the associate, don't you think?

In addition to this type of general support, you'll also want to have a separate system which defines the role of the associate and how he fits into your firm. In Chapter 11, Michael referred to this as an associate architect development system, and if you're even toying with the idea of hiring more architects, this is one system you don't want to be without.

Just like the job description you've created for other positions in your office, an associate architect development system will outline the basic duties and responsibilities assigned to new associates when they walk through the door. You weren't just going to let them grab a project and run with it, were you? The development system provides not only the goals and measures that they will be held to, but also the tools they'll need to succeed.

It includes everything from their pay scale and experience requirements to the methods that they should use to document a project, contact a client, and yes, report on their hours for each project. It gives you the ability to monitor their growth and more importantly, gives them the means of measuring their own performance, which is a positively empowering way to do business.

Since you were shooting for something more profound than just another architectural practice anyway, "empowering" is certainly a great place to start.

Why would you hire an associate architect?

- Grow your business—more clients, more income
- Expand your expertise to offer services in area of associate's experience
- Share your work load so you can pursue other interests
- Permit you to take longer holidays, more often

What needs to be in place before you hire an associate?

1. A written outline of why your business needs an associate architect

2. A written list of responsibilities and accountabilities of an associate—a position description in detail

3. A recruiting and hiring system to increase chances of hiring the best available candidate

4. A clearly stated strategic objective of the firm and view for the future

5. A complete set of systems for how your business is run

6. An orientation system that will incorporate your associate into the firm in a meaningful way

7. A system for you to monitor and measure the associate's performance

8. A way to reward the associate for extraordinary performance

9. A long-term plan for the role of the associate in the firm.

If these elements are in place and shared with the prospective associate, the chances of their success in your firm will be enhanced. The candidate will know what to expect and what he/she is getting into, and you will be able to quickly know whether you have the chosen the correct candidate for your associate architect. ✤

On the Subject of Estimating

Michael E. Gerber

The way a Chihuahua goes about eating a dead elephant is to take a bite and be very present with that bite. In spiritual growth, the definitive act is to take one step and let tomorrow's step take care of itself.
—William H. Houff, *Infinity in Your Hand: A Guide for the Spiritually Curious*

One of the greatest weaknesses of architects is accurately estimating how long appointments will take and then scheduling their clients accordingly. *Webster's Collegiate Dictionary* defines estimate as "a rough or approximate calculation." Anyone who has visited a potential jobsite knows that those estimates can be rough indeed.

Do you want to see someone who gives you a rough approximation? What if your architect gave you a rough approximation of when you would receive your architectural drawings for your new office building?

The fact is, we can predict many things we don't typically predict. For example, there are ways to learn the truth about people who come in complaining about HVAC or TI's. Look at the steps of the process. Most of the things you do are standard, so develop a step-by-step system and stick to it.

In my book *The E-Myth Manager*, I raised eyebrows by suggesting that doctors eliminate the waiting room. Why? You don't need it if you're always on time. The same goes for an architectural firm. If you're always on time, then your clients don't have to wait. What if you were to eliminate design estimations from the process or not do them for free? Begin in the first phone call to set clients' expectations and their perception of value.

What if an architect made this promise: On time, every time, as promised, or we pay for it.

"Impossible!" architects cry. "Each client is different. We simply can't know how long each appointment will take."

Do you follow this? Since architects believe they're incapable of knowing how to organize their time, they build a business based on lack of knowing and lack of control. They build a business based on estimates.

I once had an architect ask me, "What happens when someone calls about an architect and you discover their property is actually too small for the project they desire to be completed?

This is your chance to demonstrate professionalism. Point out the problem, acknowledge the new opportunity to serve and stick to your meeting schedule. Provide your insight, offer creative ideas and build rapport.

The solution is interest, attention, analysis. Try detailing what you do at the beginning of an interaction, what you do in the middle, and what you do at the end. How long does each take? In the absence of such detailed, quantified standards, everything ends up being an estimate, and a poor estimate at that. What will it take to move clients one step closer to trusting you with this portion of the home improvement project?

However, a business organized around a system has time for proper attention. It's built right into the system.

Too many architects have grown accustomed to thinking in terms of estimates without thinking about what the term really means. Is it any wonder many architectural firms are in trouble?

Enlightened architects, in contrast, banish the word estimate from their vocabulary. When it comes to estimating, just say no!

"But you can never be exact," architects have told me for years. "Close, maybe. But never exact."

I have a simple answer to that: You have to be. You simply can't afford to be inexact. You can't accept inexactness in yourself or in your architectural firm.

You can't go to work every day believing that your company, the work you do, and the commitments you make are all too complex and unpredictable to be exact. With a mindset like that, you're doomed to run a sloppy ship—a ship that will eventually sink and suck you down with it!

This is so easy to avoid. Sloppiness—in both thought and action—is the root cause of your frustrations.

The solution to those frustrations is clarity. Clarity gives you the ability to set a clear direction, which fuels the momentum you need to grow your business.

Clarity, direction, momentum—they all come from insisting on exactness.

But how do you create exactness in a hopelessly inexact world? The answer is this: You discover the exactness in your practice by refusing to do any work that can't be controlled exactly.

The only other option is to analyze the market, determine where the opportunities are, and then organize your company to be the exact provider of the services you've chosen to offer.

Two choices, and only two choices: (1) Evaluate your company and then limit yourself to the tasks you know you can do exactly, or (2) start all over by analyzing the market, identifying the key opportunities in that market, and building a company that operates exactly.

What you cannot do, what you must refuse to do, from this day forward, is to allow yourself to operate with an inexact mindset. It will lead you to ruin.

Which leads us inexorably back to the word I have been using through this book: systems.

Who makes estimates? Only architects who are unclear about exactly how to do the task in question. Only architects whose experience has taught them that if something can go wrong, it will—and to them!

I'm not suggesting that a systems solution will guarantee that you always perform exactly as promised. But I am saying that a systems solution will faithfully alert you when you're going off track, and will do it before you have to pay the price for it.

In short, with a systems solution in place, your need to estimate will be a thing of the past, both because you have organized your company to anticipate mistakes, and because you have put into place the system to do something about those mistakes before they blow up.

There's this too: To make a promise you intend to keep places a burden on you and your managers to dig deeply into how you intend to keep it. Such a burden will transform your intentions and increase your attention to detail.

With your promise comes dedication. With dedication comes integrity. With integrity comes consistency. With consistency comes results you can count on. And results you can count on mean that you get exactly what you hoped for at the outset of your company: the true pride of ownership that every architect should experience.

This brings us to the subject of clients. Who are they? Why do they come to you? How can you identify yours? And who should your clients be? But first let's see what Norbert has to say about estimating. ✤

CHAPTER
14

Is Anything Certain?

Norbert C. Lemermeyer

To be uncertain is to be uncomfortable, but to be certain is to be ridiculous.

—Chinese Proverb

For most architects, a percentage fee is the natural way to bill for services on a project. They feel that it is unnatural, charging a flat fee for services rendered, so they'll stick to their percentage billing, thank you very much; that's the way fees are intended to be. For some projects and in some situations, alternate fee arrangements may be more appropriate.

Many clients have questioned percentage billing by the architectural firms they retain, as the practice appears to reward architects for increasing construction costs in order to increase their fees. Some architectural firms are taking incremental steps away from percentage fees. Alternate fee arrangements typically involve charging a flat fee. The idea resonates much more, as clients try to adhere to tighter budgets. Ultimately it could be more profitable, if we are as good as we think we are.

Uncertainty about architectural fees has always been a major source of irritation with clients. There's nothing more disconcerting than sitting in an architect's office while he tries to increase the value of the project, seemingly to increase his fees. This often results in clients reaching out for help outside of architecture, where results can be disastrous, but the fees are certain.

Industry has been recommending the flat-fee model for years. Why? Because the flat-fee model is the only model that provides certainty not only to the client but to the architect as well. This could be a potentially win-win situation.

From the client's point of view, the flat-fee model offers the advantage of determining the exact cost of architectural fees. Clients feel more relaxed and meetings become more productive. Clients feel that the entire experience of obtaining architectural services is balanced in their favor. Using the flat-fee model, architects will no longer appear to have a financial incentive to add cost to a project to increase their fees, a practice many clients assume to be the normal way of doing business with architects.

From the architect's perspective, a flat-fee model has some distinct advantages. It simplifies the billing process and provides the architect with more time to manage the client's project, as it eliminates the need to constantly track construction costs as the basis of fees. The flat-fee model is built around efficiency. Efficiency in your operation occurs when written systems are in place at every level of your business, systems that allow technologists and other non-architectural staff to handle certain matters in a timely and cost-efficient manner.

Systems and delegations will allow you to determine an accurate cost of your services and will enable you to develop a flat-fee rate that is both realistic and competitive. There may be instances where projects take more or less time than anticipated, but they average out in the long run.

Another way to take advantage of flat-fee billing is to create "packages" by bundling services together and charging appropriate fees.

Packages can offer clients a tiered approach to services; each segment of the project is clearly identified along with a fee. The client sees the work relative to the fee for each segment and will acknowledge and appreciate the effort more. These packages can also work as a great marketing tool. Create and trademark a unique name for each level of service to distinguish your services from your competitors.

The goal here is not to nickel-and-dime the clients with charges for every little thing. It may create animosity and diminishes referrals. Bundle your services so that some extra services are within the fees. Some clients may abuse this approach, but the hassles you eliminate, the referrals you generate, and the goodwill you create will be well worth it.

Develop a means to give clients a guarantee. No, you can't control the outcome of pricing of unforeseen situations, but you can guarantee the level of service you'll provide, such as providing regular updates and returning phone calls within a certain amount of time. Some areas of architecture may prohibit this particular practice, but use it where appropriate. Some clients may abuse this service, too, but imagine the excitement if word got out that you offered a guarantee!

Many business have been doing guarantees for years, so why not architectural firms? Service guarantees may look much like a gimmick, but they remain a powerful tool for the entrepreneurial architectural firm. Guarantees give clients a sense of control in an otherwise uncontrollable matter, and they shift some of the risk to the architectural firm, making the relationship more advantageous and, therefore, more appealing to the client.

A major revolution is taking place throughout the world today. Businesses of all sizes are committed to a customer-centric environment. The architectural profession needs to become part of that revolution.

Do everything possible to create a level of certainty in the minds of your clients. Bundle your service and offer flat fees. Provide your clients with a service guarantee. Make all your communications to clients in understandable, plain English. Write with the client's interests in mind, not using jargon to make people think you're smart. Break concepts down so that clients understand what's happening on their project. It will eliminate unnecessary phone calls to the office and keep clients informed and happy.

In my office over the past three years we have systematically asked our clients for feedback on our services at various touch points throughout the project. Touch points are natural interface points with the client such as:

- at the signing of the Client/Architect agreement
- at completion and approval of the design program
- at completion of the schematic design phase
- at completion of the design development
- at completion and approval of construction documents
- after tendering/pricing
- at billing points
- at job site meetings throughout the construction period

Open-ended questions will provide clients an opportunity to tell you about their perceptions and how you can improve your services. The following are typical questions to ask at touch points:

- How do you like our services on the project up to now?
- Do our services meet with your expectations? If not, why?
- How could we improve our services?
- What questions do you have about what's coming up on the project?

The responses to these questions are gold. Until we started this practice in our office, we were often at odds with our clients at the end of a project. Not only were we at odds, but we didn't know why. We guessed but never knew for sure. After the project was over we didn't have an opportunity to fix what we were doing wrong, and clients believed they overpaid for the services.

With the feedback we are now getting during these touch points, we are able to explain to our clients how our fees are relevant to the services rendered. They begin to understand that our fees are fair and well-earned, bringing true value to the project.

Our system of regularly asking our clients for feedback, listening to what they are telling us and adjusting how we provide service has had the single largest impact on our relationships with our clients in helping them understand that our fees are relative to our service.

Remember, systems, predictability, consistency and efficiency result in an architectural practice that is on the fast track to success. ❧

On the Subject of Clients

Michael E. Gerber

*Some clients I see are actually draining into their bodies the diseased
thoughts of their minds.*

—Zachary T. Bercovitz, *Wisdom for the Soul:
Five Millennia of Prescriptions for Spiritual Healing*

When it comes to the business of architecture, the best definition of *clients* I've ever heard is this: very special people
who drive most architects crazy.

Does that work for you?

After all, clients rarely show any appreciation for what an architect has to go through to do the job as promised. Don't they always
think the price is too high? And don't they focus on problems, broken
promises, and the mistakes they think you make, rather than all the
ways you bend over backward to give them what they need?

Do you ever hear other architects voice these complaints? More
to the point, have you ever voiced them yourself? Well, you're not

alone. I have yet to meet an architect who doesn't suffer from a strong case of client confusion.

Client confusion is about

- what your clients really want;
- how to communicate effectively with your clients;
- how to keep your clients truly happy;
- how to deal with client dissatisfaction; and
- whom to call client.

Confusion 1: What Your Clients Really Want

Your clients aren't just people, they're very specific kinds of people. Let me share with you the six categories of clients as seen from the E-Myth marketing perspective: (1) tactile clients, (2) neutral clients, (3) withdrawal clients, (4) experimental clients, (5) transitional clients, and (6) traditional clients.

Your entire marketing strategy must be based on with which type of client you are dealing. Each of the six client types spends money on architects for very different, and identifiable, reasons. These are:

- Tactile clients get their major gratification from interacting with other people.
- Neutral clients get their major gratification from interacting with inanimate objects (computers, cars, information).
- Withdrawal clients get their major gratification from interacting with ideas (thoughts, concepts, stories).
- Experimental clients rationalize their buying decisions by perceiving that what they bought is new, revolutionary, and innovative.
- Transitional clients rationalize their buying decisions by perceiving that what they bought is dependable and reliable.
- Traditional clients rationalize their buying decisions by perceiving that what they bought is cost-effective, a good deal, and worth the money.

In short:

If your clients are tactile, you have to emphasize the people of your business.

If your clients are neutral, you have to emphasize the technology of your business.

If your clients are withdrawal clients, you have to emphasize the idea of your business.

If your clients are experimental clients, you have to emphasize the uniqueness of your business.

If your clients are transitional, you have to emphasize the dependability of your business.

If your clients are traditional, you have to talk about the financial competitiveness of your business.

What your clients want is determined by who they are. Who they are is regularly demonstrated by what they do. Think about the clients with whom you do business. Ask yourself: In which of the categories would I place them? What do they do for a living?

If your client is a mechanical engineer, for example, it's probably safe to assume he's a neutral client. If another one of your clients is a cardiologist, she's probably tactile. Accountants tend to be traditional, and software engineers are often experimental.

Having an idea about into which categories your clients may fall is very helpful in figuring out what they want. Of course, there's no exact science to it, and human beings constantly defy stereotypes. So don't take my word for it. You'll want to make your own analysis of the clients you serve.

Confusion 2: How to Communicate Effectively with Your Clients

The next step in the client satisfaction process is to decide how to magnify the characteristics of your business that are most likely to appeal to your preferred category of client. That begins with what marketing people call your *positioning strategy*.

What do I mean by *positioning* your business? You position your business with words—a few well-chosen words to tell your clients exactly what they want to hear. In marketing lingo, those words are called your USP, or *unique selling proposition.*

For example, if you are targeting tactile clients (those who love people), your USP could be: "Architects—We offer a lifetime of quality service, with a capital "A"." No questions asked." If you are targeting experimental clients (those who love new, revolutionary things), your USP could be: "Sky High —we have all the angles you need for your next purchase!"

In other words, when they choose to schedule an appointment with you, they can count on both your services and equipment to be on the cutting edge of the architectural industry.

Is this starting to make sense? Do you see how the ordinary things most architects do to get clients can be done in a significantly more effective way?

Once you understand the essential principles of marketing the E-Myth way, the strategies by which you attract clients can make an enormous difference in your market share.

Confusion 3: How to Keep Your Clients Happy

Let's say you've overcome the first three confusions. Great. Now how do you keep your clients happy?

Very simple—just keep your promise! And make sure your clients know you kept your promise every step of the way.

In short, giving your clients what they think they want is the key to keeping your clients (or anyone else, for that matter) really happy.

If your clients need to interact with people (high touch, tactile), make certain they do.

If they need to interact with things (high tech, neutral), make certain they do.

If they need to interact with ideas (in their head, withdrawal), make certain they do.

And so forth.

At E-Myth, we call this your client fulfillment system. It's the step-by-step process by which you do the task you've contracted to do and deliver what you've promised—on time, every time.

But what happens when your clients are not happy? What happens when you've done everything I've mentioned here and your client is still dissatisfied?

Confusion 4: How to Deal with Client Dissatisfaction

If you have followed each step up to this point, client dissatisfaction will be rare. But it can and will still occur—people are people, and some people will always find a way to be dissatisfied with something. Here's what to do about it:

- Always listen to what your clients are saying. And never interrupt while they're saying it.

- After you're sure you've heard all of your client's complaint, make absolutely certain you understand what she said by phrasing a question such as: "Can I repeat what you've just told me, Ms. Harton, to make absolutely certain I understand you?"

- Secure your client's acknowledgment that you have heard her complaint accurately.

- Apologize for whatever your client thinks you did that dissatisfied her, even if you didn't do it!

- After your client has acknowledged your apology, ask her exactly what would make her happy.

- Repeat what your client told you would make her happy, and get her acknowledgment that you have heard correctly.

- If at all possible, give your client exactly what she has asked for.

You may be thinking, *But what if my client wants something totally impossible?* Don't worry. If you've followed my recommendations to the letter, what your client asks for will seldom seem unreasonable.

Confusion 5: Whom to Call Clients

At this stage, it's important to ask yourself some questions about the kind of clients you hope to attract to your company:

- With which types of clients would you most like to do business?
- Where do you see your real market opportunities?
- Whom would you like to work with, provide services to, and position your business for?

To what category of client are you most drawn? A tactile client for whom people are most important? A neutral client for whom the mechanics of how you do business is most important? An experimental client for whom cutting-edge innovation is important? A traditional client for whom low cost and certainty of delivery are absolutely essential?

Once you've defined your ideal clients, go after them. There's no reason you can't attract these types of people to your architectural firm and give them exactly what they want.

In short, it's all up to you. No mystery. No magic. Just a systematic process for shaping your business's future. But you must have the passion to pursue the process. And you must be absolutely clear about every aspect of it.

Until you know your clients as well as you know yourself.

Until all your complaints about clients are a thing of the past.

Until you accept the undeniable fact that client acquisition and client satisfaction are more science than art.

But unless you're willing to grow your business, you better not follow any of these recommendations. Because if you do what I'm suggesting, it's going to grow.

That brings us to the subject of growth. But first, find out what Norbert has to say about clients.❖

How Does Your Client Love You?

Norbert C. Lemermeyer

Almost all of our relationships begin and most of them continue as a form of mutual exploitation, a mental or physical barter, to be terminated when one or both parties run out of goods.

—W.H. Auden

T he relationship between architect and client is a peculiar thing. The client entrusts you to handle some of his biggest expenditures, so it is imperative to know how and what the expectations are in order to be trusted with these expenditures. Technical and design competence are not the only qualities that are required for satisfied clients. Each client has unique needs and wants in the course of completing a project.

Clients are the lifeline of your firm, yet these same clients are also often the most annoying thorn in your side. It can be a love-hate relationship.

What's really interesting is not that this relationship exists, but that both parties seem content in allowing it to continue in its current

111

state. When was the last time you gave any real effort to improving your relationships with existing clients?

When most architects talk about building their practices, they frequently focus on attracting new clientele. They believe that as long as their marketing efforts provide a steady stream of new clients, their businesses will grow and thrive. But limiting your client development activities to finding and engaging new clients can be a huge mistake.

I realized I needed to abandon the mindset that clients represent a one-time transaction, and substitute it with the notion that each client has a lifetime value. Of course, I needed to continue to bring new clients into the firm. That's just good business, but a large chunk of the client development budget must be spent on retention of existing clients, not attracting new ones. Here's why:

- The costs of attracting a new client are five times greater than the cost of retaining an existing client.
- The return on investment for client retention activities is ten times higher than for new client marketing.
- Existing clients can be the best source of new client referrals, out-producing even the best marketing efforts.
- Leveraging the potential of existing clients quickly increases bottom-line profits.

The best tool for attracting new business is your existing client base. Trouble is, in the typical architectural firm, the importance of existing clients is frequently underestimated or overlooked altogether.

Architects often pin their hopes of building a successful business on expensive marketing campaigns while ignoring the potential that surrounds them—their existing clients. Take a look at the roster of existing clients and ask: What additional services will each client likely need in the future? What are the possible referral sources? To which groups or centers of influence could each client introduce me? Calculate the potential revenue from each existing client. You'll be amazed to discover the value of what you already have and can easily leverage.

For example, an architect recognized that his average client was worth more than $125,000 in additional business over the course of a lifetime. This means an architect can think of a client's value to the business in the short term by looking only at the value of the immediate services provided, or choose to focus on the lifetime value of the client. It's a choice. If there is a change in perspective, the architect can be rewarded handsomely.

Changing how existing clients are valued will alter the entire dynamic of the client/architect relationship and reshape marketing endeavors. For example, how much would you pay in client acquisition costs to acquire a new client that costs $50,000 versus $10,000 to retain an existing client?

Once the initial contact has been made, it is the job of the architect to nurture and develop a solid, sustainable relationship with the client. To do that, remember one thing: it doesn't matter what the architect wants; it's what the client wants that counts.

Figuring out what clients want isn't as hard as it seems. For starters, they want to be heard. They want a little understanding, maybe some compassion and even empathy for their current situation. They want to feel that you appreciate their business and that you respect them as human beings. Oh, and they'd also like to trust that your architectural expertise can help solve their problems. Is that too much to ask?

In an architectural office that's primarily concerned with billings, it probably is too much to ask. In your firm, the new "revolutionary" firm, this type of service is the norm.

You'll need systems in place to ensure that's the case because more than 90 percent of your dissatisfied clients will simply never return, and they won't tell you why they left. They will, however, tell others—every chance they get.

Customer satisfaction studies continue to report that each dissatisfied client will tell between ten and twenty people about their bad experience. That's ten to twenty potential new clients that you'll never see. Keep your clients happy and you'll reap the benefits of the same word-of-mouth network that could have quickly tanked your reputation. That means new clients for the firm without spending a marketing penny. How's that for efficiency!

Keeping clients happy is relatively easy in most cases. Simply maintaining regular communication can go a long way in fostering client satisfaction. Add some honesty and integrity and you've got a winning combination. It's harder to sue someone for malpractice when that person continuously goes the extra mile for you, whether they made a mistake or not.

If you want to build an architectural business that will last for the long term, you must have a system in place that attracts new clients to your roster while providing continued service to your existing list of clients. This is the only way to build the kind of client loyalty that leads to an inexhaustible source of referrals. This system begins with communication. Regular contact with all your clients is essential. Start with systematic contact several times a year and build on that. Touch base at least once a month.

Don't be boring about it. Look for creative and interesting ways to communicate, such as client newsletters, greeting cards for birthdays, anniversaries, holidays, etc. Have you got the idea? Plan special client appreciation events or an open house. Take clients bowling, stage an event in their honor, and make it fun.

Clients want to bond with you and your firm. They want to see you as people, not faceless professionals. Many architects think that it diminishes their credibility to be "people" rather than professionals, but the only way to build trust is to let clients get to know who you are. You don't have to be the distant and arrogant architect in order to impress people and get business. That's a myth that's costing you revenue.

Since we're talking about talking, communication with clients needn't be exclusively about architecture. Talk about yourself, hobbies, vacations, or even funny incidents that happen to you or your staff.

Clients want to know what's going on in their project, but beyond that, communications can be more casual. They already know that you're competent; if they didn't, you wouldn't be their architect.

What they need is to see that you're human—that you have a dog or like to run or volunteer once a month at the local shelter.

These are the qualities that draw people to you, not prestigious degrees and awards. If you doubt this theory, then think about a doctor with a poor bedside manner. Despite all his medical expertise, you won't hesitate to find someone else.

Don't you suppose the architect-client relationship works the same way? Here's a test. If you have a newsletter that you send to clients, insert an article about your dog, your vacation, an achievement of your kids, or something memorable about your staff, and track which items your clients talk about. We guarantee the next time they come in or call you on the phone they will comment about your vacation, your dog, or that funny incident in the office well before they mention the new zoning by-law that affects their project. Communicating systematically in this way will be enormously rewarding. Own the field in your community, because everyone else is still living in the dark ages.

Remember, the value of your business is determined by your clients, your connection to them, and most importantly, the systems you have in place to continue and enhance those relationships. Look at how you can improve both the initial contact with each client as well as their subsequent interactions to ensure they always feel connected, cared about, and important to the firm.

Our Experience

In my office we have developed a system that helps maintain and strengthen relationships with our clients.

As I outlined in Chapter 14, with our touch point system, we regularly ask our clients for feedback. We ask prepared questions, listen to the answers, and act upon what we hear by adjusting our services to better work for our clients. Over the years, by listening to our client's feedback, we have adjusted our services to better suit their needs. Also, we have learned that one style of service does not work for all clients. We need to get feedback continuously so that we are on track with all our clients all the time.

Our touch point system involves each and every staff member. First of all, our staff gets direct feedback so they can adjust their work and client interface to suit. The clients appreciate that they receive exactly what they ask for and that their requests are above company policy. By empowering our staff to ask our clients for feedback, they feel a more integral part of our mission to serve the clients. They also get to hear firsthand when a client compliments their work.

In the past, we have always felt strongly about our design and technical capabilities to perform the work on time and on budget. However, we were not always in tune with the clients' needs. Inadvertently, we lost some clients without knowing why. Now, because we systematically connect with and listen to clients, we know what we must do to maintain clients from one project to the next. We also know, if a client's demands are too onerous, when to say thanks but no thanks.

Superior client fulfillment based on tight systems will lead to continuing client satisfaction, not to mention that it will generate a few referrals in the process. The result of all of this will be consistent, sustainable growth, bringing you a very big step closer to your vision of what an architectural practice should be. ❧

On the Subject of Growth

Michael E. Gerber

Growth is the only evidence of life.
—John Henry Newman, *Apologia Pro Vita Sua*

The rule of business growth says that every business, like every child, is destined to grow. Needs to grow. Is determined to grow.

Once you've created your architectural firm, once you've shaped the idea of it, the most natural thing for it to do is to . . . grow! And if you stop it from growing, it will die.

Once an architect has started a business, it's his or her job to help it grow. To nurture it and support it in every way. To infuse it with these qualities:

- Purpose
- Passion
- Will

- Belief
- Personality
- Method

As your company grows, it naturally changes. And as it changes from a small company to something much bigger, you will begin to feel out of control. News flash: That's because you are out of control.

Your company has exceeded your know-how, sprinted right past you, and now it's taunting you to keep up. That leaves you two choices: Grow as big as your company demands you grow, or try to hold your company at its present level—at the level you feel most comfortable.

The sad fact is that most architects do the latter. They try to keep their company small, securely within their comfort zone. Doing what they know how to do, what they feel most comfortable doing. It's called playing it safe.

But as the company grows, the number, scale, and complexity of tasks will grow too until they threaten to overwhelm the architect. More people are needed. More space. More money. Everything seems to be happening at the same time. A hundred balls are in the air at once.

As I've said throughout this book: Most architects are not entrepreneurs. They aren't true businesspeople at all, but technicians suffering from an entrepreneurial seizure. Their philosophy of coping with the workload can be summarized as "just do it" rather than figuring out how to get it done through other people using innovative systems to produce consistent results.

Given most architects' inclination to be the master juggler in their companies, it's not surprising that as complexity increases, as work expands beyond their ability to do it, and as money becomes more elusive, they are just holding on, desperately juggling more and more balls. In the end, most collapse under the strain.

You can't expect your company to stand still. You can't expect your company to stay small. A company that stays small and depends on you to do everything isn't a company—it's a job!

Yes, just like your children, your business must be allowed to grow, flourish, change, and become more than it is. In this way, it will match your vision. And you know all about vision, right? You better. It's what you do best!

Do you feel the excitement? You should. After all, you know what your company is but not what it can be.

It's either going to grow or die. The choice is yours, but it is a choice that must be made. If you sit back and wait for change to overtake you, you will always have to answer no to this question: Are you ready?

That brings us to the subject of change. But first, let's see what Norbert has to say about growth. ❧

CHAPTER
18

Growth Beyond Architecture

Norbert C. Lemermeyer

Why stay on earth unless we grow.

—Robert Browning

It is the nature of any business to grow. With first one client and then another, new projects come along and new ideas are born; the business begins to expand. The systems and processes discussed in previous chapters are designed to help the business grow effortlessly and efficiently.

Since you're reading this book, my guess is that you've come to that fork in the road. Your business is ready to grow; are you ready to grow with it? Then it's time to make that leap and change the way you see your firm. A well-run architectural practice on a track for growth must exist as a separate entity from its architect-owner. Although the owner may work in the business with clearly defined tasks, the practice itself is your creation, one with a life of its own. The practice itself is the product shaped and molded, and it should be able to stand whether you're around to run it or not.

This not the case with most practices. They are neither created nor operated as businesses, but as revolving completely around the personality and capacity limits of the architect. If the architect stops working, takes a vacation, or wants to retire some day, the practice revenue stops, too. In the real world, there's very little difference between a regular architect with a job and the owner of an architectural practice. The old way of doing things just simply won't work anymore. As the way you live and work continues to evolve, so must your architectural firm.

The percentage fee is giving way to alternative methods of fee calculation. Staffing is being leveraged so that technologists and other paraprofessionals are taking over as many duties in the firm as possible, allowing the architect to spend more time developing business strategies and doing the work that only a licensed architect can do.

It's not just fee models and staffing that are changing. Leveraging the work product through automation is now accepted by a profession that is known for its risk-adverse attitude toward technology, which is embedded in its soul. Like in any business, time is money to the architectural profession. The more time it takes to perform routine tasks, the greater the cost to the firm. Reducing the time it takes to perform routine tasks saves money and frees up time to perform additional tasks, thereby creating an opportunity to gain even more revenue.

Utilizing technology means upgrading computer hardware and finding time-saving software applications to make work more efficient. It may mean outsourcing business tasks to experts or lower-wage workers for routine tasks. It means looking at new marketing opportunities in the online world. It means embracing the web with an interactive website that provides quality content and answers to those commonly asked questions.

It means looking at creating visibility with a blog that shares your wisdom and allows people to see who you are and what you have to offer. It may mean using new online advertising methods to generate clients. Social media sites like Facebook, Twitter, and LinkedIn are opening up a new world for architects to maintain relationships with existing clients, gain referral sources, attract new clients, and grow. These are new models that give us a glimpse of what the future of architectural services may look like.

We are the beneficiaries of the greatest technological revolution this world has ever seen. Ignore the transformational changes that are occurring all around you, and your practice will wither and die. Old-school thinking argues that it shouldn't be this way. A new day has dawned. Technology today provides sophisticated and efficient ways of completing routine tasks, tracking client matters, generating custom documents, collaborating online, and communicating the results instantly. With the rise of the personal and networked computer and the growth of the Internet, you would think every architect in practice today would embrace this new way of doing business, but it's not always true.

In many architectural firms, antiquated technology systems are in play. Very few practices have comprehensive accounting and billing systems, document-generating software, or relational databases to track everything. Instead, yellow legal pads, a rolodex, giant day planners, and bulging manila folders are the currency of most firms. As a result, a regular architectural firm scene is a staff person scurrying from desk to desk asking if anyone has seen the Johnson project file.

By the dawn of the twenty-first century, new digital technology made it possible for architectural firms and architectural professionals to engage in the practice of architecture via cyberspace. This new practice approach utilizes Internet computing for the delivery of architectural services. The market is huge. Research shows the next generation of clients is much more comfortable interacting online with minimal face-to-face contact and very little of the traditional hand- holding from the more traditional architectural model.

The demands of the consumer will cause these issues to eventually be resolved. One thing remains clear: the power of innovation must permeate the architectural firm that is to grow. There are only two aspects to any successful business—innovation and marketing, both of which will inevitably lead to growth. Most architects don't even own basic contact-management software that holds client information, and tracks all communications with staff, clients, and vendors, or software that can generate marketing reports and deliver an instant dashboard of the vital signs of the business.

This kind of technology provides the tools that will keep you on the fast track to growth. Leveraging these tools, plus systems and trained support staff can guarantee that the firm will not be caught by surprise when conditions change.

With times rapidly changing, architects with traditional skills and attitudes are on shaky ground in this new emerging economy. The ones who could imagine a better way to acquire clients and deliver architectural services are the new stars.

An architect in a large firm recently told me about layoffs at his firm. Who was being axed? Architects who were used to just showing up and having work handed to them were the first to go because the work just wasn't there. Those who had the ability to imagine new services, new opportunities, and new ways to recruit work were being retained. They were untouchable.

Just being an average accountant, lawyer, architect, or assembly-line worker is not the ticket it used to be. As Daniel Pink, the author of *A Whole New Mind*, puts it, "We are in a world in which more and more average work can be done by a computer, robot or talented foreigner faster, cheaper and just as well."

The practice of architecture is a business, and that in a business there is no status quo. You are either winning or losing; things are either getting better or getting worse. Like life itself, you are either growing or decaying.

Most architects don't have their fingers on the pulse of their businesses. They are too busy "working in the business" on tactical tasks instead of "working on the business," engaged in strategic work. They discover too late that business is dying.

There simply is no substitute for having systems in place to provide the kinds of critical information you need on things like marketing activity, conversion of clients, architectural work produced, and financial information. The key to a successful, growing practice is to be eternally vigilant. Pay attention to detail, examine, and act on the information provided by your systems, and adjust whenever and wherever it becomes necessary.

You must know where you're going. To get there, your goal must be to go from a practice that is dependent upon you, to a business you run.

Up to this point, we've certainly covered a lot of ground. I've tried to lay out a vision that will transform your practice into a real business. What is preventing you from taking decisive action to redesign your architectural firm, along with your life?

My Experience

It took me two runs at it to change. The first time I attempted to make a change in my architectural practice was thirteen years ago. I began to make changes to my firm according to the E-Myth. By this time I'd been in business for over fifteen years. When I read about the E-Myth, it promised me a new start and so I followed the advice.

Within the first year, I experienced unprecedented success. The firm contracted many new clients and we began to grow. From working on the business, I again began working in the business. Even though we were financially much more successful than ever before, I was still working long hours and weekends with very little in the way of holidays. Except for the money, I was at the same place as when I began with the E-Myth.

Upon examining the business, I had only partially converted the firm. So six years ago, I re-launched the E-Myth practice in my firm. This time I committed to completely change the way my firm was run. I enrolled in the online E-Myth Mastery program and as I went through the program, I converted all aspects of the firm step-by-step as outlined in the program. This was a huge commitment and a cataclysmic change to my firm, which had been in business for over twenty-five years. I was determined to either retire or change.

Just when we should have experienced an impact from converting the firm from Oldco into Newco, the economy in our region went into recession. In the past when we'd experience a recession, we have to lay off staff and reduce our expenses. Due to our preparedness and the systems, we were able to maintain our status quo. We cut back marginally on our expenses and didn't have any layoffs of our staff. The slow time was an opportunity to tune up our systems and processes for how we ran the office. This gave us time to train and educate the staff.

New forecasts show the economy is on the upswing. We look forward to this time with the systems at the ready and a staff trained in our practices and systems. I am confident as I have never been before. Should we require additional systems to successfully complete the work, to improve running of the firm, and to adjust the business as required, we are confident we have the tools and the will to know how to do it.

We have made more changes to how we practice architecture in the past five years than in the preceding twenty-five. I can see a future where change is the only constant. To begin with, the changes are slow, but as the systems are put into place the momentum of change begins to pick up. Due to the efficiency of using systems, we gain the time needed to continue making changes. Rather than being fearful about change, we now embrace change.

Are all our changes successful? No. As new changes come on stream they are evaluated and cancelled if they do not serve their intended purpose.

The most important lesson I learned, in making this transformation to my business in accordance with the E-Myth, is that we live in a time where change is never ending. The questions must constantly be asked: What can be done to improve the firm? What systems need to be put into place to produce the work more efficiently? How can we improve the use of our staff? How can we better use the tools of our times—the Internet, social media, and new marketing strategies?

There are many different answers, but the truth is, the biggest barrier to success is the one seen in your mirror every day. Is this a surprise? As architects we have been trained to see only the issues and problems, that is, why things can't work. You tell yourself every reason why this won't work in your practice. The firm is too big. It's too small. You live in a rural area. You live in an urban setting. You're too old. You're too young. Chances are if you've made it this far, you are able to get a glimpse of what possibilities are just around the corner. Hold on to those dreams and imagine what your architectural firm could become. ❧

CHAPTER
19

On the Subject
of Change

Michael E. Gerber

There is nothing permanent except change.
———Heraclitus of Ephesus, *Lives of the Philosophers*

S
o your company is growing. That means, of course, that it's also changing. Which means it's driving you and everyone in your life crazy.

That's because, to most people, change is a diabolical thing. Tell most people they've got to change, and their first instinct is to crawl directly into a hole. Nothing threatens their existence more than change. Nothing cements their resistance more than change. Nothing!

Yet for the past thirty-five years, that's exactly what I've been proposing to small business owners: the need to change. Not for the sake of change itself, but for the sake of their lives.

I've talked to countless architects whose hopes weren't being realized through their company, whose lives were consumed by work, who slaved increasingly longer hours for decreasing pay, whose dissatisfaction grew as their enjoyment shriveled, whose company had become the worst job in the world, whose money was out of control, and whose employees were a source of never-ending hassles, just like their clients, their bank, and, increasingly, even their family.

More and more, these architects spent their time alone, dreading the unknown and anxious about the future. And even when they were with people, they didn't know how to relax. Their minds were always on the job. They were distracted by work, by the thought of work. By the fear of falling behind.

And yet, when confronted with their condition and offered an alternative, most of the same architects strenuously resisted it. They assumed that if there were a better way of doing business, they already would have figured it out. They derived comfort from knowing what they believed they already knew. They accepted the limitations of being an architect, the truth about people, or the limitations of what they could expect from their clients, their employees, their architect subcontractors, their bankers—even their family and friends.

In short, most architects I've met over the years would rather live with the frustrations they already have than risk enduring new frustrations.

Isn't that true of most people you know? Rather than opening up to the infinite number of possibilities life offers, they prefer to bind their lives at respectable limits. After all, isn't that the most reasonable way to live?

I think not. I think we must learn to let go. I think that if you fail to embrace change, it will inevitably destroy you.

Conversely, by opening yourself to change, you give your architectural firm the opportunity to get the most from your talents.

Let me share with you an original way to think about change, about life, about who we are and what we do. About the stunning notion of expansion and contraction.

Contraction vs. Expansion

"Our salvation," a wise man once said, "is to allow." That is, to be open, to let go of our beliefs, to change. Only then can we move from a point of view to a viewing point.

That wise man was Thaddeus Golas, the author of a small, powerful book titled *The Lazy Man's Guide to Enlightenment* (Seed Center, 1971).

Among the many inspirational things he had to say was this compelling idea:

"The basic function of each being is expanding and contracting. Expanded beings are permeable; contracted beings are dense and impermeable. Therefore each of us, alone or in combination, may appear as space, energy, or mass, depending on the ratio of expansion to contraction chosen, and what kind of vibrations each of us expresses by alternating expansion and contraction. Each being controls his [or her] own vibrations."

In other words, Golas tells us that the entire mystery of life can be summed up in two words: expansion and contraction. He goes on to say:

"We experience expansion as awareness, comprehension, understanding, or whatever we wish to call it.

"When we are completely expanded, we have a feeling of total awareness, of being one with all life.

"At that level we have no resistance to any vibrations or interactions of other beings. It is timeless bliss, with unlimited choice of consciousness, perception, and feeling.

"When a (human) being is totally contracted, he is a mass particle, completely imploded.

"To the degree that he is contracted, a being is unable to be in the same space with others, so the contraction is felt as fear, pain, unconsciousness, ignorance, hatred, evil, and a whole host of strange feelings.

"At an extreme (of contraction), (a human being) has the feeling of being completely insane, of resisting everyone and everything, of being unable to choose the content of his consciousness.

"Of course, these are just the feelings appropriate to mass vibration levels, and he can get out of them at any time by expanding, by letting go of all resistance to what he thinks, sees, or feels."

Stay with me here. Because what Golas says is profoundly important. When you're feeling oppressed, overwhelmed, or exhausted by more than you can control—*contracted*, as Golas puts it—you can change your state to one of expansion.

According to Golas, the more contracted we are, the more threatened we are by change; the more expanded we are, the more open we are to change.

In our most enlightened—that is, open—state, change is as welcome as non-change. Everything is perceived as a part of ourselves. There is no inside or outside. Everything is one thing. Our sense of isolation is transformed to a feeling of ease, of light, and of joyful relationship with everything.

As infants, we didn't even think of change in the same way, because we lived those first days in an unthreatened state. Insensitive to the threat of loss, most young children are only aware of what is. Change is simply another form of what is. Change just is.

However, when we are in our most contracted—that is, closed—state, change is the most extreme threat. If the known is what I have, then the unknown must be what threatens to take away what I have. Change, then, is the unknown. And the unknown is fear. It's like being between trapezes.

To the fearful, change is threatening because things may get worse.

To the hopeful, change is encouraging because things may get better.

To the confident, change is inspiring because the challenge exists to improve things.

If you are fearful, you see difficulties in every opportunity. If you are fear-free, you see opportunities in every difficulty.

Fear protects what I have from being taken away. But it also disconnects me from the rest of the world. In other words, fear keeps me separate and alone.

Here's the exciting part of Golas's message: With this new understanding of contraction and expansion, we can become completely attuned to where we are at all times.

If I am afraid, suspicious, skeptical, and resistant, I am in a contracted state. If I am joyful, open, interested, and willing, I am in an expanded state. Just knowing this puts me on an expanded path. Always remembering this, Golas says, brings enlightenment, which opens me even more.

Such openness gives me the ability to freely access my options. And taking advantage of options is the best part of change. Just as there are infinite ways to greet a client, there are infinite ways to run your company. If you believe Thaddeus Golas, your most exciting option is to be open to all of them.

Because your life is lived on a continuum between the most contracted and most expanded—the most closed and most open—states, change is best understood as the movement from one to the other, and back again.

Most small business owners I've met see change as a thing in itself, as something that just happens to them. Most experience change as a threat. Whenever change shows up at the door, they quickly slam it. Many bolt the door and pile up the furniture. Some even run for their gun.

Few of them understand that change isn't a thing in itself, but rather the manifestation of many things. You might call it the revelation of all possibilities. Think of it as the ability at any moment to sacrifice what we are for what we could become.

Change can either challenge us or threaten us. It's our choice. Our attitude toward change can either pave the way to success or throw up a roadblock.

Change is where opportunity lives. Without change we would stay exactly as we are. The universe would be frozen still. Time would end.

At any given moment, we are somewhere on the path between a contracted and expanded state. Most of us are in the middle of the journey, neither totally closed nor totally open. According to Golas, change is our movement from one place in the middle toward one of the two ends.

Do you want to move toward contraction or toward enlightenment? Because without change, you are hopelessly stuck with what you've got.

Without change,

- we have no hope;
- we cannot know true joy;
- we will not get better; and
- we will continue to focus exclusively on what we have and the threat of losing it.

All of this negativity contracts us even more, until, at the extreme closed end of the spectrum, we become a black hole so dense that no light can escape.

Sadly, the harder we try to hold on to what we've got, the less able we are to do so. So we try still harder, which eventually drags us even deeper into the black hole of contraction.

Are you like that? Do you know anybody who is?

Think of change as the movement between where we are and where we're not. That leaves only two directions for change: either moving forward or slipping backward. We either become more contracted or more expanded.

The next step is to link change to how we feel. If we feel afraid, change is dragging us backward. If we feel open, change is pushing us forward.

Change is not a thing in itself, but a movement of our consciousness. By tuning in, by paying attention, we get clues to the state of our being.

Change, then, is not an outcome or something to be acquired. Change is a shift of our consciousness, of our being, of our humanity, of our attention, of our relationship with all other beings in the universe.

We are either "more in relationship" or "less in relationship." Change is the movement in either of those directions. The exciting part is that we possess the ability to decide which way we go—and to know in the moment which way we're moving.

Closed, open; open, closed. Two directions in the universe. The choice is yours.

Do you see the profound opportunity available to you? What an extraordinary way to live!

Enlightenment is not reserved for the sainted. Rather, it comes to us as we become more sensitive to ourselves. Eventually, we become our own guides, alerting ourselves to our state, moment by moment: open . . . closed . . . open . . . closed.

Listen to your inner voice, your ally, and feel what it's like to be open and closed. Experience the instant of choice in both directions.

You will feel the awareness growing. It may be only a flash at first, so be alert. This feeling is accessible, but only if you avoid the black hole of contraction.

Are you afraid that you're totally contracted? Don't be—it's doubtful. The fact that you're still reading this book suggests that you're moving in the opposite direction.

You're more like a running back seeking the open field. You can see the opportunity gleaming in the distance. In the open direction.

Understand that I'm not saying that change itself is a point on the path; rather, it's the all-important movement.

Change is in you, not out there.

What path are you on? The path of liberation? Or the path of crystallization?

As we know, change can be for the better or for the worse.

If change is happening inside of you, it is for the worse only if you remain closed to it. The key, then, is your attitude—your acceptance or rejection of change. Change can be for the better only if you accept it. And it will certainly be for the worse if you don't.

Remember, change is nothing in itself. Without you, change doesn't exist. Change is happening inside each of us, giving us clues to where we are at any point in time.

Rejoice in change, for it's a sign you are alive.

Are we open? Are we closed? If we're open, good things are bound to happen. If we're closed, things will only get worse.

According to Golas, it's as simple as that. Whatever happens defines where we are. How we are is where we are. It cannot be any other way.

For change is life.

Charles Darwin wrote, "It is not the strongest of the species that survive, nor the most intelligent, but the one that proves itself most responsive to change."

The growth of your architectural firm, then, is its change. Your role is to go with it, to be with it, to share the joy, embrace the opportunities, meet the challenges, and learn the lessons.

Remember, there are three kinds of people: (1) those who make things happen, (2) those who let things happen, and (3) those who wonder what the hell happened. The people who make things happen are masters of change. The other two are its victims.

Which type are you?

The Big Change

If all of this is going to mean anything to the life of your company, you have to know when you're going to leave it. At what point, in your company's rise from where it is now to where it can ultimately grow, are you going to sell it? Because if you don't have a clear picture of when you want out, your company is the master of your destiny, not the reverse.

As we said earlier, the most valuable form of money is equity, and unless your business vision includes your equity and how you will use it to your advantage, your company will forever consume you.

Your company is potentially the best friend you ever had. It is your company's nature to serve you, so let it. If, however, you are not a wise steward, if you do not tell your company what you expect from it, it will run rampant, abuse you, use you, and confuse you.

Change. Growth. Equity.

Focus on the point in the future when you will take leave of your company. Now reconsider your goals in that context. Be specific. Write them down.

Skipping this step is like tiptoeing through earthquake country. Who can say where the fault line is waiting? And who knows exactly when your whole world may come crashing down around you?

Which brings us to the subject of time. But first, let's see what Norbert has to say regarding change. ❧

Changes

Norbert C. Lemermeyer

Taking a new step, uttering a new word, is what people fear most.
—Fyodor Dostoevsky

R adical changes will envelop the practice of architecture during the next ten years. Envisioning the impact of technology will change the function of the architect. For the conservative architect, the future is bleak; for the progressive architect, exciting new opportunities will emerge. The architectural profession has never looked more flexible than it does today and what we're seeing now is just the tip of the iceberg.

Where you once needed an architect, now you just need the CAD draftsman and an engineer to stamp the drawings. But buyer beware. Online advisors have streamlined a number of practice areas, offering consumers a seemingly complete summary of building materials, building systems, and off-shore graphics services of any idea at the click of the mouse. It's all online and it doesn't cost a fraction of what a consumer would pay you; in fact, some of it doesn't cost anything at all. Design-it-yourself programs are available to anyone who owns a computer, giving him the power to think he can replace the architect.

What's sad about this new trend is that architects are being cut out of the deal, consumers are being hoodwinked, and it's only going to get worse. Travel agents, accountants, and even bank tellers have already fallen prey to our technology-driven society. We've replaced face-to-face contact with online banking, virtual shopping carts, and tax preparation software, all of which are open 24/7 and you don't even need an appointment to get started.

Booksellers now have to compete with handheld digital book readers that can download that newest bestseller for you in less than a minute, and real estate agents get to compete with online databases that can filter, categorize, compare, and show any property in any place at any time. What makes us think the architectural profession will be safe?

The technology facilitating these changes continues to plow forward, evolving and growing into something bigger and more magnificent than we ever imagined. It was once fairly easy to deny the lasting power and effectiveness of computers as another passing fad; that day is long gone and it's time to face the music. The technology is here, it won't be going away, and it will only become more powerful. It's changing the way we practice architecture. Yet in the face of all this change, how can we be so incredibly optimistic about the future?

Because change means opportunity. Opportunities to grow, to learn, and to achieve something that perhaps no one has envisioned before are available. To take advantage of these opportunities, you'll need to be open to the changes that are coming, changes that will require you to rethink the way you approach your practice. Exciting, isn't it?

You have a unique advantage that other industries don't have; not only do you know the changes are coming, but you can also see how they will likely play out. This knowledge puts you in the very coveted position of being able to lead the change rather than just follow along with everyone else. Isn't that what you wanted for your practice? To be the firm that sets the pace, while your competitors try to keep up?

To make this transformation, you'll need to wear a new hat, one of a visionary who is no longer constrained by the architectural firm stereotypes you're leaving behind.

Instead of looking for ways to increase your billings, look for ways to increase the value you offer to clients. For example, replace your static website (assuming you have one), with something that's interactive, engaging, and informative. Don't just recite the credentials of your staff; instead, give answers to commonly asked questions. Explain the differences between types of construction contracts, for instance, or list the criteria for creating a facility evaluation.

Include a blog that not only highlights the achievements of your firm but also explains recent changes in architecture, in layman's terms no less, so that someone looking for this information feels that they "got value" from your site.

Want to combat all those online do-it-yourselfers? Explain how that can get you into trouble in many situations, and then offer package alternatives (we discussed this earlier, remember?) that are priced reasonably enough to make it worth consumers' consideration.

After all, if they were willing to purchase online assistance from a non-professional, don't you think they'd be willing to pay for advice that came from a reasonably priced consultation from someone who knows what they're doing? Be the firm that redefines how an architectural firm should be. Create brochures that enable clients to come prepared for your meeting and send these out with a letter confirming their next appointment.

Have preprinted packages that cover common concerns in your area of practice and give these to clients when the meeting is over. Include CDs or pamphlets and perhaps even a small gift card to your local coffee shop so that clients can go out afterward and discuss the ideas you've presented to them.

Build relationships by continuing to touch base with both prospects and clients, offering new services and packages that reflect
not just what you're willing to sell but that also address what the
client actually wants to buy. Does this mean the days of big money
fees are over? Absolutely not! You can still be the Ritz-Carlton of
architectural firms. In fact, that's exactly what we want you to be.

But remember, what makes the Ritz "The Ritz" is not its hefty
price, but the service-rich experience you have when you stay
there. Mints on your feather pillows, valet service, car service, fruit
baskets, continental breakfast—the list just goes on and on.

No one thinks twice about paying their higher-than-average
fee because hey, it's The Ritz. Your architectural firm should be
the same way. Like a four-star hotel, you should wrap your clients
in extraordinary service, service that goes beyond the acceptable
minimum and sets a new standard for other firms to try and match.

It's not the client/architect agreement, the construction documents, the bidding process, or the technical research, it's the
unique process that you create in your firm to methodically take a
client from where they are to where they want to be in a transfor-
mative way. Big money can be charged for this process, and believe
us when we say that happy clients will be glad to pay your fees.

So, while we're recommending creating packages and services
that highlight price, we don't want that to be your main focus.
Quite the contrary. Minimize the issue of price, and instead emphasize the value of relationship, expertise, and client experience.

This is where the "results in advance" concept can really pay
off. Give your prospects a taste of what they're looking for without
any risk or cost to them. It could be a free report or an educational
seminar or some other service or event that moves them further
toward their goal.

Now that we're on a roll, let's not stop here! Revamp your
marketing strategy to represent the new and improved firm you're
now creating. Build those social media profiles we keep talking
about and learn what it means to tweet and post. Build a Facebook
page, update your "status" often, and interact with the rest of the

digital world. Use your social media presence to share information, promote your services, and connect with the masses because that's really what the digital age is all about—connecting with the masses, not just an elite few

Create a newsletter that can be subscribed to from your web site for free and include a special report as a free gift for subscribing. What kind of special report, you ask? How about "10 Top Secrets to Construction Projects" or "The Five Essential Things Every Client Should Know About Architectural Service." The topics are endless; just look at your area of practice and think about what kind of information could be useful.

Learn about search engine optimization, article marketing, and even viral videos to drive traffic to your web site and thus, your firm. If you think you'll never master all this new technology, fear not, because there are people out there who are happy to handle this kind of thing for you. Designers, programmers, writers—there are thousands of experienced and knowledgeable professionals who are able and willing to hold your hand and walk you into the digital age.

In fact, you may employ people with some of these talents already and just don't know it. After all, just because you haven't embraced the new technology doesn't mean the members of your staff are living in the dark ages, too. Which means you can leverage your staff or outsource this piece of your marketing puzzle altogether. The choice is up to you.

Our Experience

In our office, to date, we have only employed a few of the suggestions made in this chapter. We have employed a practice of unexpected service to clients. Clients are given something extraordinary, above and beyond what is written and expected in the Client/Architect Agreement.

In the past, it has been our experience that our client's trust in us has waned during the construction phase of the project. During this time we spent less time with them, while the contractor was taking our place explaining the design and details through our drawings. These explanations often pointed out his strengths and our weaknesses or perceived weaknesses. Thus, our reputation suffered during this phase of our services, no thanks to the contractor and thanks to our inattention.

One practice we have adopted now that we never did in the past, is to bring the client to the construction site and give them a detailed tour of the site. On this tour we explain in detail what is currently being done relative to the drawings and their vision. The engineers are present to outline the mechanical and electrical systems in detail along with answering questions the client might have. The tradesmen are available to review with the client their challenges and how they are being overcome.

Since we've begun the practice of guided tours of the construction site, although it takes valuable time, we have gained a new closeness to our clients and, rather than going backward, our reputation, in the eyes of our clients, has strengthened.

A second practice we now utilize is the touch-point process. Throughout the project, at regular intervals we obtain feedback through questions to the clients about our service.

- How do you like our services on the project up to now?
- Do our services meet with your expectations? If not, why?
- How could we improve our services?
- What questions do you have about what's coming up on the project?

We listen to the answers and act upon what we hear. Since we've begun this process, we have gleaned valuable information about our client service. Although some of the answers are difficult and costly to comply with, we find that we can offer these services at an extra cost which the client is willing to pay. Some of the feedback we receive are items easily added to our service at no cost to us and to great appreciation from the client. A satisfied client is a repeat client.

In the past, we assumed all clients needed and wanted a standard service from architects. Since we've begun the practice of questioning our clients about our service, we found a wide disparity in client expectations and how they want their services. Some of these answers were subtleties that would have never been picked up unless we specifically asked. Now that we know these items, we can more easily give them good service (which we always do) in a manner that is more suitable to them. A satisfied client is a repeat client.

Since we have begun these and other practices, we are encouraged to continue to look for additional ways to adjust our services to clients. This continuous search for new and better ways has now become part of a culture of dealing with our clients, of always looking for ways to fine-tune our services. Now more than ever before we feel that we are on track with client service. Most importantly, clients have favorably responded to our new practices. We feel a closeness to clients like we've never felt before in our long history in architecture.

You'll be taking a big step in the right direction, positioning your firm to be a leader in the new ways of architecture. You'll be embracing the change before the change leaves you, and your firm, in the dust. ✤

CHAPTER
21

On the Subject
of Time

Michael E. Gerber

*Take time to deliberate; but when the time for action arrives, stop
thinking and go in.*

—Andrew Jackson

I'm running out of time!" architects often lament. "I've got to learn
how to manage my time more carefully!"

Of course, they see no real solution to this problem. They're
just worrying the subject to death. Singing the architecture blues.

Some make a real effort to control time. Maybe they go to time
management classes, or faithfully try to record their activities during
every hour of the day.

But it's hopeless. Even when architects work harder, even when
they keep precise records of their time, there's always a shortage of
it. It's as if they're looking at a square clock in a round universe.
Something doesn't fit. The result: The architect is constantly
chasing work, money, life.

And the reason is simple. Architects don't see time for what it really is. They think of time with a small "t," rather than Time with a capital "T."

Yet, Time is simply another word for your life. It's your ultimate asset, your gift at birth—and you can spend it any way you want. Do you know how you want to spend it? Do you have a plan?

How do you deal with Time? Are you even conscious of it? If you are, I bet you are constantly locked into either the future or the past. Relying on either memory or imagination.

Do you recognize these voices? "Once I get through this, I can have a drink . . . go on a vacation . . . retire." "I remember when I was young and being an architect was satisfying."

As you go to bed at midnight, are you thinking about waking up at seven a.m. so you can get to the office by eight a.m. so you can go to lunch by noon, because your software/pesticide people will be there at 1:30 p.m. and you've got a full schedule and a new client scheduled for 2:30?

Most of us are prisoners of the future or the past. While ping-ponging between the two, we miss the richest moments of our life—the present. Trapped forever in memory or imagination, we are strangers to the here and now. Our future is nothing more than an extension of our past, and the present is merely the background.

It's sobering to think that right now each of us is at a precise spot somewhere between the beginning of our Time (our birth) and the end of our Time (our death).

No wonder everyone frets about Time. What really terrifies us is that we're using up our life and we can't stop it.

It feels as if we're plummeting toward the end with nothing to break our free fall. Time is out of control! Understandably, this is horrifying, mostly because the real issue is not time with a small "t" but Death with a big "D."

From the depths of our existential anxiety, we try to put Time in a different perspective—all the while pretending we can manage it. We talk about Time as though it were something other than what it is. "Time is money," we announce, as though that explains it.

But what every architect should know is that Time is Life. And Time ends! Life ends! The big, walloping, irresolvable problem is that we don't know how much Time we have left.

Do you feel the fear? Do you want to get over it?

Let's look at Time more seriously.

To fully grasp Time with a capital "T," you have to ask the Big Question: How do I wish to spend the rest of my Time?

Because I can assure you that if you don't ask that Big Question with a big "Q," you will forever be assailed by the little questions. You'll shrink the whole of your life to this time and the next time and the last time—all the while wondering, *What time is it?*

It's like running around the deck of a sinking ship worrying about where you left the keys to your cabin.

You must accept that you have only so much Time; that you're using up that Time second by precious second. And that your Time, your life, is the most valuable asset you have. Of course, you can use your Time any way you want. But unless you choose to use it as richly, as rewardingly, as excitingly, as intelligently, as intentionally as possible, you'll squander it and fail to appreciate it.

Indeed, if you are oblivious to the value of your Time, you'll commit the single greatest sin: You will live your life unconscious of it passing you by.

Until you deal with Time with a capital "T," you'll worry about time with a small "t" until you have no Time—or life—left. Then your Time will be history—along with your life.

I can anticipate your question: If Time is the problem, why not just take on fewer clients? Well, that's certainly an option, but probably not necessary. I know an architect with a company that sees three times as many clients as the average, yet he doesn't work long hours. How is it possible?

This architect has a system. Roughly 50 percent of what needs to be communicated to clients is "downloaded" to the office staff. By using this expert system, the employees can do everything the architect or his subcontractors would do—everything that isn't architect-dependent.

Be vs. Do

Remember when you asked yourself, "What do I want to be when I grow up?" It was one of our biggest concerns as children.

Notice that the question isn't, "What do I want to *do* when I grow up?" It's "What do I want to *be?*"

Shakespeare wrote, "To be or not to be" not "To do or not to do."

But when you grow up, people always ask you, "What do you do?" How did the question change from being to doing? How did we miss the critical distinction between the two?

Even as children, we sensed the distinction. The real question we were asking was not what we would end up doing when we grew up, but *who* we would be.

We were talking about a life choice, not a work choice. We instinctively saw it as a matter of how we spend our Time, not what we do in time.

Look to children for guidance. I believe that as children we instinctively saw Time as life and tried to use it wisely. As children, we wanted to make a life choice, not a work choice. As children, we didn't know—or care—that work had to be done on time, on budget.

Until you see Time for what it really is—your life span—you will always ask the wrong question.

Until you embrace the whole of your Time and shape it accordingly, you will never be able to fully appreciate the moment.

Until you fully appreciate every second that comprises Time, you will never be sufficiently motivated to live those seconds fully.

Until you're sufficiently motivated to live those seconds fully, you will never see fit to change the way you are. You will never take the quality and sanctity of Time seriously.

And unless you take the sanctity of Time seriously, you will continue to struggle to catch up with something behind you. Your frustrations will mount as you try to snatch the second that just whisked by.

If you constantly fret about time with a small "t," then big-"T" Time will blow right past you. And you'll miss the whole point, the real truth about Time: You can't manage it; you never could. You can only live it.

And so that leaves you with these questions: How do I live my life? How do I give significance to it? How can I be here now, in this moment?

Once you begin to ask these questions, you'll find yourself moving toward a much fuller, richer life. But if you continue to be caught up in the banal work you do every day, you're never going to find the time to take a deep breath, exhale, and be present in the now.

So let's talk about the subject of work. But first, let's find out what Norbert has to say about time. ❧

CHAPTER 22

How Will You Spend Your Time?

Norbert C. Lemermeyer

Ah! The clock is always slow; it is later than you think.

—Robert Service

Time is not on your side.

Michael E. Gerber teaches a sobering lesson in this chapter when he warns that "time" and "life" are essentially synonymous, and that the "time" you have left is really the "life" you have left. Once you accept that fact, time takes on new significance.

Most architects don't manage their time very well, and don't use it productively. I've been in business for over thirty years and count myself into that group that manages time poorly. Our approach to life is that we are managed by the events that surround us and the fires we have to put out each day. Time manages us, and we wind up with a nice, but unimaginative picture of a life that follows a well-traveled path and lacks the magnificence of the masterpiece it could have been and that we dreamed it to be when we began.

Walter M. Bortz says, "We live short and die long," and the urgency of getting on with what we are meant to do with this one short life increases with each passing day.

We're not just talking about professional accomplishments, but rather about being the kind of person that you're intended to be in every area of life. We're talking about a life that is rich in a variety of experiences, including helping the kids with their homework, spending quality time with your significant other, caring for elderly parents, dealing with chores in the home, and spending time with friends. The point of this all lies in a fundamental challenge to make our lives a creative work of art.

Our philosophy is centered on a simple, but powerful, technique called "time blocking." Time blocking involves consistently setting aside time for the high-priority activities in both your work life and your personal life.

You cannot be effective in your professional life if your inner reserves are depleted. Periodically, you need to make time to recharge your batteries and give yourself an energy boost. Block time for exercise, meditation, relaxation, or recreation, and don't forget to carve out time for your family and friends. Treat appointments with yourself just as respectfully as you would those with others.

At work, block the time you will need to do the work of an architect/owner. Consider this: Schedule a block of time each day to focus on building your business. Use this uninterrupted time to plan or work on special projects, develop marketing plans, train and develop your staff, or simply to learn something new that will help you grow your business. This will yield rich dividends in short order. Just be sure you don't compromise this time with extraneous activities, or surrender it altogether because of the pressures of the moment, like putting out fires.

One of the keys to managing your time more effectively is to determine how you are currently spending your time. A time log is an excellent way to do this. Keep a time log for a week. After doing it, some important insights will become evident about how you could manage your time better. Understanding where your time is spent is the first step in changing some bad habits.

Here's how to keep a time log. Throughout each day of your selected week, record the time whenever you start and stop any activity in which you become involved. Consider logging time for the entire day, not just the work part of the day. Remember to be as detailed as possible. It is not at all unlikely that you will log a hundred entries or more per day.

Once you have collected the data, sort it into general categories (e.g., client meetings, document preparation, email, web surfing, phone calls, administrative tasks, marketing, research, eating, spending time with your significant other, attending meetings, playing with your kids, and yes, even going to the bathroom). Calculate the percentage of time you spent in each activity. At the end of the week, determine what percentage of your time is being spent on each activity.

If you're like most people, you'll find that the biggest time waster of them all is the evil but necessary email. No question that it's an excellent tool when judiciously used, but most people check their email incessantly all day long on the off chance that they've missed something. Set up a schedule for checking email that only involves a few select times during the day, and let that schedule be widely known. You'll be surprised at how much more you will be able to accomplish, and how little you missed.

Here are a few other suggestions that will help you become more efficient and, as a result, have more time to balance your work with every other part of your life .

- Analyze your time log and determine what you are doing that could be delegated, and then delegate it. This will help you determine what work should be handed over to someone else. If there's anything you're doing that could be delegated for less than your hourly rate, then delegated it should be.

- Determine what your highest and best use of your time is, based on your strengths, and see what percentage of your time is actually being spent in this area.

- Develop a plan to make sure everyone around you does not waste your time, and then stick to it. Interruptions are common in an architectural firm, but they can be dramatically reduced by effective staff meetings where questions are raised and answered, rather than asked throughout the workday. Properly planned "stand-up meetings" with key staff during the week can also eliminate interruptions and increase productivity.

• Ask your staff to log their activities for a week as well. They may be surprised to learn how little time they are actually spending on work-related projects. Studies have concluded that the average office worker only performs about 1.5 hours of actual work each day. The balance of their workday is spent socializing, taking coffee breaks, engaging in non-business-related communication, as well as other non-work tasks. (Remember, this is intended to be a lesson in self-discovery, not an opportunity to find fault. Allow staff members to learn from this activity without feeling that they are the subjects of a management time study.)

Now, we know you've heard some of these ideas before, and we also know you probably wrote them off. But before you make that same mistake again, look at your own time log and consider what it's telling you.

The information contained in your time log could be the key to changing the way you experience your day. Like the athlete who reviews a video after a game, your time log allows you to play the part of spectator and see where you need work.

Our Experience

Upon completion of the time log, we developed four tools that together helped us all manage our time better than ever before. They are now engrained in the culture of our office:

• Annual personal target and education plan
• Monthly production plan and results
• Weekly staff meeting
• The day plan

The annual personal target and education plan helps each individual staff member and his/her manager together work to raise their production level based on 200 working days per year, and decide how to best use them efficiently for personal growth for themselves and their employer. This plan is set each fiscal year and is reviewed monthly at an employee development meeting, becoming the center-piece in the year-end employee evaluation.

The monthly production plan sets out production targets for each project so each staff member is completely aware of and can commit to the firm's expectations on a monthly basis. The production targets are reviewed at the end of the month with discussions on targets missed and why they were missed and what can be done to improve production and productivity in the office. Production is the bread and butter of the firm. It's the most important indicator measuring the health of the company, and it points out how time is or is not being wisely used. Team discussions are held for input on how production targets could be more readily achieved.

Each week a staff meeting is held where projects, challenges, exchanges of information, and successes are discussed. These meetings, some say, are a waste of time. We believe and have measured that these meetings prevent time-wasting questions, interruptions, and other inefficiencies that were once common in our office. The time spent in these meetings prevents confusion, misunderstandings, and, in fact, results in better use of time.

Every staff member, every day, plans their work in a day plan, a written, measurable description of tasks to be completed. This is done daily before any other tasks are begun. A half hour is allowed for this exercise. During this time, staff members can set up meetings with other staff members, discuss issues of mutual concern, or talk to their managers as required. Every new staff member is at first reluctant to complete this required plan, but is soon converted and says they could no longer get along without it. Some say they plan their weekends at home using the day plan, as it helps them do more in their free time.

These tools have been set up customized for our method of doing things; however, they have been inspired and modeled by Michael E. Gerber's E-Myth's advice. Once we began to use these tools and modified them to best serve our company, our time crisis situations were reduced to near zero. As these tools became the culture in our office, we had more time to work on our business rather than in our business, and got more production per man. These tools/systems have led to a continuous cycle of improvement and growth. These tools, in conjunction with other processes, ensure that we get the best return on our most coveted commodity—time.

Using tools like these also allows you to ensure that your time, and thus, your life, is being spent the way you want it to be spent—that the things you consider to be your highest priorities are actually getting their due. Because when you put first things first, you begin making full use of your greatest asset: the time you have left. ✤

On the Subject of Work

Michael E. Gerber

*As we learn we always change, and so our perception. This changed
perception then becomes a new Teacher inside each of us.*

—Hyemeyohsts Storm

In the business world, as the saying goes, the entrepreneur
knows something about everything, the technician knows
everything about something, and the switchboard operator just
knows everything.

In an architectural firm, architects see their natural work as the
work of the technician. The Supreme Technician. Often to the exclu-
sion of everything else.

After all, architects get zero preparation for working as a manager
and spend no time thinking as an entrepreneur—those just aren't
courses offered in today's schools and colleges of planning and design.
By the time they own their own architectural firm, they're just doing
it, doing it, doing it.

At the same time, they want everything—freedom, respect, money. Most of all, they want to rid themselves of meddling bosses and start their own company. That way they can be their own boss and take home all the money. These architects are in the throes of an entrepreneurial seizure.

Architects who have been praised for their amazing clinical skills believe they have what it takes to run an architectural firm. It's not unlike the plumber who becomes a contractor because he's a great plumber. Sure, he may be a great plumber—but it doesn't necessarily follow that he knows how to build a company that does this work.

It's the same for an architect. So many of them are surprised to wake up one morning and discover that they're nowhere near as equipped for owning their own company as they thought they were.

More than any other subject, work is the cause of obsessive-compulsive behavior by architects.

Work. You've got to do it every single day.

Work. If you fall behind, you'll pay for it.

Work. There's either too much or not enough.

So many architects describe work as what they do when they're busy. Some discriminate between the work they could be doing as architects and the work they should be doing as architects.

But according to the E-Myth, they're exactly the same thing. The work you could do and the work you should do as an architect are identical. Let me explain.

Strategic Work vs. Tactical Work

Architects can do only two kinds of work: strategic work and tactical work.

Tactical work is easier to understand because it's what almost every architect does almost every minute of every hour of every day. It's called getting the job done. It's called doing business.

Tactical work includes drawing, scaling, design, repairing, replacing, and seeing clients.

The E-Myth says that tactical work is all the work architects find themselves doing in an architectural firm to avoid doing the strategic work.

"I'm too busy," most architects will tell you.

"How come nothing goes right unless I do it myself?" they complain in frustration.

Architects say these things when they're up to their ears in tactical work. But most architects don't understand that if they had done more strategic work, they would have less tactical work to do.

Architects are doing strategic work when they ask the following questions:

- Why am I an architect?
- What will my company look like when it's done?
- What must my company look, act, and feel like for it to compete successfully?
- What are the key indicators of my company?

Please note that I said architects ask these questions when they are doing strategic work. I didn't say these are the questions they necessarily answer.

That is the fundamental difference between strategic work and tactical work. Tactical work is all about answers: How to do this. How to do that.

Strategic work, in contrast, is all about questions: What company are we really in? Why are we in that company? Who specifically is our company determined to serve? When will I sell this company? How and where will this company be doing business when I sell it? And so forth.

Not that strategic questions don't have answers. Architects who commonly ask strategic questions know that once they ask such a question, they're already on their way to envisioning the answer. Question and answer are part of a whole. You can't find the right answer until you've asked the right question.

Tactical work is much easier because the question is always more obvious. In fact, you don't ask the tactical question; instead, the question arises from a result you need to get or from a problem you need to solve. Billing a client is tactical work. Designing a pond in a backyard is tactical work. Firing an employee is tactical work. Diagnosing plant disease is tactical work.

Tactical work is the stuff you do every day in your practice. Strategic work is the stuff you plan to do to create an exceptional company/business/enterprise.

In tactical work, the question comes from out there rather than in here. The tactical question is about something outside of you, whereas the strategic question is about something inside of you.

The tactical question is about something you need to do, whereas the strategic question is about something you want to do. Want versus need.

If tactical work consumes you,

- you are always reacting to something outside of you;
- your company runs you; you don't run it;
- your employees run you; you don't run them; and
- your life runs you; you don't run your life.

You must understand that the more strategic work you do, the more intentional your decisions, your business, and your life become. Intention is the byword of strategic work.

Everything on the outside begins to serve you, to serve your vision, rather than forcing you to serve it. Everything you need to do is congruent with what you want to do. It means you have a vision, an aim, a purpose, a strategy, an envisioned result.

Strategic work is the work you do to design your business, to design your life.

Tactical work is the work you do to implement the design created by strategic work.

Without strategic work, there is no design. Without strategic work, all that's left is keeping busy.

There's only one thing left to do. It's time to take action. And we'll do that right after Norbert gives us his views on work. ✤

CHAPTER 24

The Other Work

Norbert C. Lemermeyer

Thunder is good, thunder is impressive, but it is lightening that does the work.

—Mark Twain

One of the most difficult jobs for us architects is to stop doing the work we do every day, long enough to engage in work we have never done before. This is what Michael E. Gerber calls "working *on* the business" as opposed to "working *in* the business."

It sounds good in theory, but getting an architect to actually put down working on projects so he can talk about brainstorming for the future is next to impossible. It reminds us of the Civil War general, in the now-famous cartoon, as he oversees his troops during a heated gun battle. Standing next to those soldiers firing the old nineteenth-century rifles is a salesman pointing to the new, automatic Gatling gun. But the general can't be bothered; the caption reads, "Not now, can't you see I'm busy!"

Like the Gatling gun, strategic work will completely change how your firm fights the battles each and every day. Often architects are stressed out about having no time, yet are engaged in countless everyday activities from taking routine phone calls to acting as the firm's IT guy when a computer problem arises. Some architects believe they are the only ones qualified to order office supplies or proof the letterhead on new stationery. One experienced architect insisted that he make the coffee every morning and pick up the daily mail!

Strategic work in this area requires that you examine all the tasks in your firm and delegate everything that does not require the architect/owner's attention to someone else in the office. The key to making this work is a delegation system that makes sure the things that need to get done are accomplished by a properly trained staff.

By taking these principles to heart, we were able to revolutionize our office by creating and installing systems that were managed by well-trained technologists, systems that took the burden off the architect and redistributed the workload in a more efficient manner. There was a fear that relinquishing control would diminish the client experience, yet what actually happened was that service improved and the staff was energized.

The unexamined belief that many jobs in the office must be done by architects has ruled our profession. One day we asked, "Why?" It was the tyranny of tradition. Other industries and professions outside of architectural practice have been looked at for inspiration. If well-trained nurses can provide quality medical care in a physician's office, why can't we do the same as architects! In fact, patients never thinks twice about the services a nurse provides before they get to see the doctor.

It's all about creating new client expectations, one of the many benefits of strategic work. Once we really understood the nature of strategic work, it changed everything. In the last chapter, Michael noted that while tactical work was all about answers, strategic work is all about questions.

These questions examine the "why" behind a particular task or function rather than just the "how." Michael also noted that when architects ask these strategic questions, they are on their way to "envisioning" the answers. This is where we really want you to put your focus.

Our Experience

For years we were mired in the tyranny of tradition on how our office ran. I had worked in a relatively successful office previous to establishing my own firm. Without asking "why," I set up my office on the traditional architectural model. Before long I was doing it, doing it, and doing it, working longer and working harder each year as time went by. After reading Michael's book in 1994, I began to realize there might be another way. The transition tools took a long time, are still taking place, and will continue to change. Once we began and could see the impact of another way, we became so inspired that we continued to make changes to the traditional way. The more we asked why, the more we changed, and the more the momentum began to build.

Initially, we set aside one day per year to review how we did things. Throughout this meeting, I felt guilty, knowing I had many things to do back at the office. Out of that first meeting came modest though significant changes. These simple changes were enough to show us that asking "why" was a worthwhile exercise.

This led to having monthly meetings out of which grew the foundations of the systems that we use today. The time it takes to work on the business versus the time to work in the business is, to this day, still a conflict. But everyone realizes now that this is a necessity and brings long-term benefits. Working in the business provides short-term benefits like increasing the monthly billings. Working on the business will give long-term benefits like stability, clarity, company strength, sustainability, and many others. These benefits often take much longer to realize, and the hours working on the business are not billable.

Don't look at what your firm is now. Instead, see your firm as you'd like it to be. The only way to figure out what strategic questions to ask is to determine how far away your current practice is from the practice you've envisioned. When you can see the differences, you'll know the questions to ask, and you'll be able to see the answers as well.

The result is a whole host of new and exciting possibilities that allow you to actually create something bigger than the projects you're working on now. Your view of not only your practice, but of the architectural profession itself will be seen through a different lens. You are now the architect of a business that reflects your dreams, values, and purpose, perhaps for the first time in your career. ❧

On the Subject of Taking Action

Michael E. Gerber

Deliberation is the work of many men. Action, of one alone.
—Charles de Gaulle

I t's time to get started, time to take action. Time to stop thinking about the old company and start thinking about the new company. It's not a matter of coming up with better companies; it's about reinventing the business of architecture and design.

And the architect has to take personal responsibility for it.

That's you.

So sit up and pay attention!

You, the architect, have to be interested. You cannot abdicate accountability for the business of architecture, the administration of architecture, or the finance of architecture.

Although the goal is to create systems into which architects can plug reasonably competent people—systems that allow the company to run without them—architects must take responsibility for that happening.

I can hear the chorus now: "But we're architects! We shouldn't have to know about this." To that I say: whatever. If you don't give a flip about your company, fine—close your mind to new knowledge and accountability. But if you want to succeed, then you'd better step up and take responsibility, and you'd better do it now.

All too often, architects take no responsibility for the business of architecture but instead delegate tasks without any understanding of what it takes to do them, without any interest in what their people are actually doing, without any sense of what it feels like to be at the front desk when a client comes in and has to wait for forty-five minutes, and without any appreciation for the entity that is creating their livelihood.

Architects can open the portals of change in an instant. All you have to do is say, "I don't want to do it that way anymore." Saying it will begin to set you free—even though you don't yet understand what the company will look like after it's been reinvented.

This demands an intentional leap from the known into the unknown. It further demands that you live there—in the unknown—for a while. It means discarding the past, everything you once believed to be true.

Think of it as soaring rather than plunging.

Thought Control

You should now be clear about the need to organize your thoughts first, then your business. Because the organization of your thoughts is the foundation for the organization of your business.

If we try to organize our business without organizing our thoughts, we will fail to attack the problem.

We have seen that organization is not simply time management. Nor is it people management. Nor is it tidying up desks or alphabetizing client files. Organization is first, last, and always cleaning up the mess of our minds.

By learning how to think about the practice of architecture, by learning how to think about your priorities, and by learning how to think about your life, you'll prepare yourself to do righteous battle with the forces of failure.

Right thinking leads to right action—and now is the time to take action. Because it is only through action that you can translate thoughts into movement in the real world and, in the process, find fulfillment.

So first, think about what you want to do. Then do it. Only in this way will you be fulfilled.

How do you put the principles we've discussed in this book to work in your architectural firm? To find out, accompany me down the path once more by following these three steps:

1. **Create a story about your company.** Your story should be an idealized version of your architectural firm, a vision of what the preeminent architect in your field should be, and why. Your story must become the very heart of your company. It must become the spirit that mobilizes it, as well as everyone who walks through the doors. Without this story, your company will be reduced to plain work.

2. **Organize your company so that it breathes life into your story.** Unless your company can faithfully replicate your story in action, it all becomes fiction. In that case, you'd be better off not telling your story at all. And without a story, you'd be better off leaving your company the way it is and just hoping for the best.

Here are some tips for organizing your architectural firm:

- Identify your company's key functions
- Identify the essential processes that link those functions
- Identify the results you have determined your company will produce
- Clearly state in writing how each phase will work

Take it step by step. Think of your company as a program, a piece of software, a system. It is a collaboration, a collection of processes dynamically interacting with one another.

Of course, your company is also people.

3. **Engage your people in the process.** Why is this the third step rather than the first? Because, contrary to the advice most business experts will give you, you must never engage your people in the process until you yourself are clear about what you intend to do.

The need for consensus is a disease of today's addled mind. It's a product of our troubled and confused times. When people don't know what to believe in, they often ask others to tell them. To ask is not to lead but to follow.

The prerequisite of sound leadership is first to know where you wish to go.

And so "What do *I* want?" becomes the first question, not "What do *they* want?" In your own company, the vision must first be yours. To follow another's vision is to abdicate your personal accountability, your leadership role, your true power.

In short, the role of leader cannot be delegated or shared. And without leadership, no architectural firm will ever succeed.

Despite what you have been told, win-win is a secondary step, not a primary one. The opposite of win-win is not necessarily "they lose."

Let's say "they" can win by choosing a good horse. The best choice will not be made by consensus. Asking, "Guys, what horse do you think we should ride?" will always lead to endless and worthless discussions. By the time you're done jawing, the horse will have already left the post.

Before you talk to your people about what you intend to do in your company and why you intend to do it, you need to reach agreement with yourself.

It's important to know (1) exactly what you want, (2) how you intend to proceed, (3) what's important to you and what isn't, and (4) what you want the company to be and how you want it to get there.

Once you have that agreement, it's critical that you engage your people in a discussion about what you intend to do and why. Be clear—both with yourself and with them.

The Story

The story is paramount because it is your vision. Tell it with passion and conviction. Tell it with precision. Never hurry a great story. Unveil it slowly. Don't mumble or show embarrassment.

Never apologize or display false modesty. Look your audience in the eyes and tell your story as though it is the most important one they'll ever hear about business. Your business. The business into which you intend to pour your heart, your soul, your intelligence, your imagination, your time, your money, and your sweaty persistence.

Get into the storytelling zone. Behave as though it means everything to you. Show no equivocation when telling your story.

These tips are important because you're going to tell your story over and over—to clients, to new and old employees, to architects, to architect subcontractors, to gardeners, and to your family and friends. You're going to tell it at your church or synagogue, to your card-playing or fishing buddies, and to organizations such as local garden clubs, chambers of commerce, or local colleges and technical schools.

There are few moments in your life when telling a great story about a great business is inappropriate.

If it is to be persuasive, you must love your story. Do you think Walt Disney loved his Disneyland story? Or Ray Kroc his McDonald's story? What about Dave Smith at Federal Express? Or Debbie Fields at Mrs. Fields Cookies? Or Tom Watson Jr. at IBM?

Do you think these people loved their stories? Do you think others loved (and still love) to hear them? I daresay all successful entrepreneurs have loved the story of their business. Because that's what true entrepreneurs do. They tell stories that come to life in the form of their business.

Remember: A great story never fails. A great story is always a joy to hear.

In summary, you first need to clarify, both for yourself and for your people, your company's story. Then you need to detail the process your company must go through to make your story become reality.

I call this the business development process. Others call it reengineering, continuous improvement, reinventing your company, or total quality management.

Whatever you call it, you must take three distinct steps to succeed:

- *Innovation.* Continue to find better ways of doing what you do.
- *Quantification.* Quantify the impact of these improvements on your company.
- *Orchestration.* Orchestrate this better way of running your company so it becomes your standard, to be repeated time and again.

In this way, the system works—no matter who's using it. And you've built a company that works consistently, predictably, and systematically. It will be a company you can depend on to operate exactly as promised, every single time.

Your vision, your people, your process—all linked.

A superior architectural firm is a creation of your imagination, a product of your mind. So fire it up and get started like Norbert did. He'll tell you about it in the next chapter. ✤

26

Taking Action

Norbert C. Lemermeyer

To do crazy things, one must behave like a coachman who has let go of the reins and fallen asleep.

—Jules Renard

Recently there has been a lot of new age talk about obtaining success through the law of attraction. This law says that you attract that which dominates your thoughts. In other words, whatever holds your attention the most is what will manifest in your life.

While the power of a focused mind can't be ignored, it's the second part of this philosophy that we want to highlight, and that part is action. For anything to happen, there must be movement in the direction of your dreams. In fact, not only do we believe in action, but we encourage *massive action*.

Now to be clear, the action can't be random or haphazard. As I mentioned earlier, it's not just that you need to climb a wall; you need to climb the right wall. We believe that the first step is to immediately set aside some time away from the distractions of the office and home life, and seriously examine what it is you want, not only for your business, but also for how your business is going to serve your life.

Now I know that you've probably heard this sage advice before, but we're betting you haven't taken it to heart because here you are, still working for the business instead of having the business working for you.

We all know how that "strategy" turns out.

So this is going to be your first step in a new direction—*your* direction, to be exact. To know how to get to where you want to be, you need to know where you want to go.

Once you've established what your "big picture" will be, the next issue you'll need to tackle is to develop a game plan for getting there. Fortunately, Michael E. Gerber provided you a perfect blueprint for this project. It's your primary aim, strategic objective, and organizational strategy paradigm that he outlined in the E-Myth book.

The primary aim will guide you in setting goals and priorities for your life. The strategic objective will detail every aspect of how your practice will support those goals and priorities, giving you the life you want. It is the vivid description of every part of your firm as it will look when it's completed: What does the office look like? How many employees? What markets do you serve? What niches in those markets are you going to pursue? What is your annual revenue? What is your owner's compensation? How many days a week will you work? What is the position of your firm in the eyes of the community?

You get the idea. You need to develop a detailed picture of your future practice to which you can aspire.

The final plan of this exercise is the organizational strategy, and this answers the practical questions of what needs to get done and who is going to do it. If you're like most architects, your organizational chart will have your name in multiple places. But that little habit is going to change now, isn't it? You're going to start matching personalities and talents to functions within your firm, so that every position in your practice is filled by a person who is perfectly suited for the job. This is your chance to wipe the slate clean and start building your firm based on your very own strategic vision.

Now you're doing real entrepreneurial work. There isn't a tactic in sight at this point.

But beware! This is not a trivial project and it isn't one of those "when I get around to it" kind of jobs. It requires a clear decision and a solid intention to build the practice of your dreams, so don't be surprised if it takes several large blocks of your time spread out over several weeks.

In fact, take as long as you need to get it right. Just get started now.

And while it would seem that an office brainstorming session would be an appropriate event in this exercise, don't do it—at least, not yet.

While you're crafting your primary aim, you want it to be "all you." This is, after all, your vision of your firm. As you move to the strategic objective and organizational strategy, you can bring in the other owners or partners of the firm, if you have them. But remember, all of this strategic planning should be done in a spirit of adventure and creativity, one that addresses the big picture as a whole rather than as a checklist for micromanaging every little task in your office.

We've been where you are now. We remember the day, more than ten years ago, when we started this same process and decided to take those fundamental actions that we're asking you to take now. These actions changed our lives and our fortunes. It was the day that we finished reading the original E-Myth book by Michael E. Gerber, and realized that although we had experienced growth and success, we were operating in chaos and needed to make fundamental changes.

This is how we did it: First, we separated and worked individually on our primary aims. What did we really want for our lives? Then we came together and worked out our strategic objective, the vision of our firm, in as much detail as possible, and finally created our master organizational strategy, complete with a plan for all the essential positions.

In anticipation of all of us coming together as a firm, we provided a copy of the E-Myth book to all members of our staff and asked them to read it carefully in preparation for a firm retreat.

Following a successful offsite retreat in which everyone fully participated, we finalized our blueprint. We were now all looking at the practice with new eyes. This allowed us to refine, and in some cases to create from scratch, systems for every task in the firm. Over the years, this basic powerful formula has played itself out in our firm.

This is a necessary part of your journey; don't skip over it.

You may find that you are a little hesitant to instigate big changes in your practice. We know. We've been there. In fact, one of the biggest hurdles when embarking on this process is the paralysis that comes from the fear of making the wrong choice or taking the wrong path.

This fear usually stems from prior business decisions gone bad, and goodness knows, we don't want to walk down those roads again. But I also know, from my own personal experience as well as that of others embarking on this journey, that the decision to undertake this project turned out to be the most important business decision of their lives and mine.

It's been said that all of your problems in life can be attributed to how we file mistakes. If you can represent the past, present, and future as giant filing cabinets, then you can see how our lives are adversely affected when the wrong "file" ends up in the wrong cabinet.

That's often what we tend to do with our life experiences. Instead of placing them in the "past" filing cabinet, we tuck them away in the cabinet marked "future," where they continue to influence our every move.

Instead of looking forward to the array of possibilities that await us, we see our failures and rejections of the past staring us down, daring us to move. But move you must. The very foundation of the architectural system is changing before our eyes. No longer can we safely rely on the traditional practice models of the past. The architectural industry is changing with, or without you.

The expectations of clients in the delivery of architectural services is also under attack. Face-to-face meetings are being replaced by emails and phone calls, and as our access to digital tools continues to grow, these issues will occur far more often. The power of the Internet, along with the digital revolution, is being felt in every specialty, in every practice, in every area of the country.

The reaction to all this change will frighten some and motivate others. I prefer to be one of the latter. I see these developments as the opportunities of a lifetime for architectural firms that are prepared.

What is clear is that you are now standing on uncertain ground. The future is not written in stone and you have the option of painting it the way you see fit.

But before you can have a business that serves your needs, the work you do in your firm must leave you feeling fulfilled and energized rather than exhausted and overworked. Managing a practice by gritting your teeth and toughing it out will never give you a career that lights you up, regardless of how much money is dumped in your lap. I've found that taking the time to discover your natural strengths and talents and then delegating everything else is a recipe for a prosperous firm.

Interestingly, most architects I've met give me a blank look when I ask what it is they really like to do, because no one ever asked them that question before. They just assumed that you throw yourself at every challenge in the firm and recognize that you have to take the bad with the good.

It is not only possible for you to avoid the things you hate, but that by doing them, you're actually slowing your own progress. In our culture we have been taught to lightly acknowledge our strengths but to really "work" on our weaknesses. It happens all the time, no matter what age you are or how much money you might make. We honestly believe that our efforts should be devoted to those areas where we perform poorly. That's what "self-improvement" is all about, right?

Research shows that it's actually far more effective and productive to work on your strengths, those innate talents that are part of your natural wiring and represent the areas in which you excel. When we spend our time doing these tasks, we feel energized, not drained. We look forward to getting started, and we're never watching the clock to see when we can stop.

Identifying your talents isn't as difficult as you might think. There are two easily accessible and reasonably priced tests you can take that will quickly show you the powerful undistinguished talents that have been shaping your life since childhood.

The first is the Kolbe A Index, a test you can take online for about $50. According to the company's web site, "IQ tests tell you what you can do. Personality tests tell you what you want to do ... The Kolbe A Index measures what you WILL or WON'T do. This quick and easy 36-question instrument gives you greater understanding of your own natural instincts and allows you to begin the process of maximizing your potential."

The second test is found in a $20 book called *StrengthsFinder 2.0*, by Tom Rath. It contains the collected wisdom of thousands of interviews done by the prestigious Gallup Group. The test provides five top themes that identify your natural strengths.

According to the Gallup Group, "[O]ur studies indicate that people who *do* have the opportunity to focus on their strengths every day are *six times as likely to be engaged in their jobs and more than three times as likely to report having an excellent quality of life in general.*"

What I'm asking you to do is figure out what it is that you "want" to do and start delegating the items that don't fit with your natural talents. "Refile" those misplaced folders in your life and create a vision of possibility in your firm. Forget about the limitations of the past. Instead, use your present to create a future that truly represents what you want, not just from a business perspective but for your life as well.

So now you've heard the Story. I hope that reading this book becomes your defining moment and is the bridge you need to take you from where you are now to where you want to be—to where you deserve to be.

Now is the perfect time to create your story, tell it to others and most importantly, live it day to day.

I am confident that if you follow these principles you will get there. Of course, I am here to help. Contact me for more information and resources at www.michaelegerber.com/co-author.

One last thing. I hope that someday you'll give this book to another architect and say, "Read, re-read. It changed my life ... enjoy." ❧

AFTERWORD

Michael E. Gerber

For more than three decades, I've applied the E-Myth principles I've shared with you in this book to the successful development of thousands of small businesses throughout the world. Many have been architectural firms-architects specializing in everything from commercial building design and construction to residential city planning and zoning development.

Few rewards are greater than seeing these E-Myth principles improve the work and lives of so many people. Those rewards include seeing these changes:

- Lack of clarity—clarified
- Lack of organization—organized
- Lack of direction—shaped into a path that is clearly, lovingly, passionately pursued
- Lack of money or money poorly managed—money understood instead of coveted; created instead of chased; wisely spent or invested instead of squandered
- Lack of committed people—transformed into a cohesive community working in harmony toward a common goal; discovering each other and themselves in the process; all the while expanding their understanding, their know-how, their interest, their attention

After working with so many architects, I know that a company can be much more than what most become. I also know that nothing is preventing you from making your company all that it can be. It takes only desire and the perseverance to see it through.

In this book—another in the E-Myth Expert series—the E-Myth principles have been complemented and enriched by stories from Norbert, a real-life architect who has put these principles to use in his company. Norbert had the desire and perserverance to achieve success beyond his wildest dreams. Now you can join him.

I hope this book has helped you clear your vision and set your sights on a very bright future.

To your company!

ABOUT THE AUTHOR

Michael E. Gerber

Michael E. Gerber is the legend behind the E-Myth series of books, which includes *The E-Myth Revisited*, *E-Myth Mastery*, *The E-Myth Manager*, *The E-Myth Enterprise* and *Awakening the Entrepreneur Within*. Collectively, his books have sold millions of copies worldwide. He is the founder of In the Dreaming Room™, a 2½-day process to awaken the entrepreneur within, and Origination, which trains facilitators to assist entrepreneurs in growing "turnkey" businesses. He is chairman of the Michael E. Gerber Companies. A highly sought-after speaker and consultant, he has trained hundreds of thousands of business owners in his career. Michael lives with his wife, Luz Delia, in Carlsbad, California.

ABOUT THE CO-AUTHOR

Norbert C. Lemermeyer

Norbert's background as a technologist and designer has made him a consummate practitioner of architecture. He is a co-founder of ACM Architecture and ACM Construction Managers, and applies his touch to all projects that come through the office. Through his 40 years of experience, Norbert's architectural projects have received national recognition and have been featured in numerous trade magazines. The infusion of the E-Myth practices into his business has created new excitement and energy, to the benefit of all team members and clients.

Norbert's "just do it" attitude ensures the clients' projects end up on time and on budget. Writing and following systems for all aspects of the practice of architecture make this target of "on time and on budget" a reality.

ABOUT THE SERIES

The E-Myth Expert series brings Michael E. Gerber's proven E-Myth philosophy to a wide variety of different professional business areas. The E-Myth, short for "Entrepreneurial Myth," is simple: Too many small businesses fail to grow because their leaders think like technicians, not entrepreneurs. Gerber's approach gives small enterprise leaders practical, proven methods that have already helped transform tens of thousands of businesses. Let the E-Myth Expert series boost your professional business today!

Books in the series include:
The E-Myth Attorney
The E-Myth Accountant
The E-Myth Optometrist
The E-Myth Chiropractor
The E-Myth Financial Advisor
The E-Myth Landscape Contractor
The E-Myth Architect

Forthcoming books in the series include:
The E-Myth Real Estate Brokerage
The E-Myth Real Estate Investor
The E-Myth Insurance Store
The E-Myth Dentist
. . . and more than 300 other industries and professions

Learn more at: www.michaelegerber.com/co-author

Have you created an E-Myth enterprise? Would you like to become a co-author of an E-Myth book in your industry? Go to www.michaelegerber.com/co-author.

THE MICHAEL E. GERBER
ENTREPRENEUR'S LIBRARY
It Keeps Growing...

Thank you for reading another E-Myth Vertical book.

Who do you know who is an expert in their industry?

Who has applied the E-Myth to the improvement of their
practice as Norbert Lemermeyer has?

Who can add immense value to others in his or her industry
by sharing what he or she has learned?

Please share this book with that individual and share that individual with us.

❧

We at Michael E. Gerber Companies are determined to transform the state
of small business and entrepreneurship worldwide. *You can help.*

To find out more, email us at Michael E. Gerber Partners, at
gerber@michaelegerber.com.

To find out how *YOU* can apply the E-Myth to *YOUR* practice,
contact us at gerber@michaelegerber.com.

Thank you for living your Dream, and changing the world.

Michael E. Gerber, Co-Founder/Chairman
Michael E. Gerber Companies™
Creator of The E-Myth Evolution™
P.O. Box 131195, Carlsbad, CA 92013
760-752-1812 O • 760-752-9926 F
gerber@michaelegerber.com
www.michaelegerber.com

Join The Evolution^{SM}

Attend the Dreaming Room Trainings
www.michaelegerber.com/dreaming-room

For Your Entrepreneurial Experience
www.michaelegerber.com/entrepreneur-experience

Awaken the Entrepreneur Within You
www.michaelegerber.com/facilitator-training

Listen to the Michael E. Gerber Radio Show
www.blogtalkradio.com/michaelegerber

Watch the latest videos
www.youtube.com/michaelegerber

Connect on LinkedIn
www.linkedin.com/in/michaelegerber

Connect on Facebook
www.facebook.com/MichaelEGerberCo

Follow on Twitter
http://twitter.com/michaelegerber

CPSIA information can be obtained
at www.ICGtesting.com
Printed in the USA
BVHW032136221218
536261BV00002B/16/P